THE HEALTHY MATCHA COOKBOOK

Energizing and Lean Green Tea–Inspired Dishes

MIRYAM QUINN-DOBLAS, MS, RD
CREATOR OF EATGOOD4LIFE.COM

T0058196

Skyhorse Publishing

Copyright © 2015 by Miryam Quinn-Doblas
Photographs copyright © 2015 by Miryam Quinn-Doblas
First paperback edition, 2020.

All rights reserved. No part of this book may be reproduced in any manner without the express written consent of the publisher, except in the case of brief excerpts in critical reviews or articles. All inquiries should be addressed to Skyhorse Publishing, 307 West 36th Street, 11th Floor, New York, NY 10018.

Skyhorse Publishing books may be purchased in bulk at special discounts for sales promotion, corporate gifts, fund-raising, or educational purposes. Special editions can also be created to specifications. For details, contact the Special Sales Department, Skyhorse Publishing, 307 West 36th Street, 11th Floor, New York, NY 10018 or info@skyhorsepublishing.com.

Skyhorse® and Skyhorse Publishing® are registered trademarks of Skyhorse Publishing, Inc.®, a Delaware corporation.

Visit our website at www.skyhorsepublishing.com.

10 9 8 7 6 5 4 3 2 1

Library of Congress Cataloging-in-Publication Data is available on file.

Cover design by Daniel Brount
Cover photo by Miryam Quinn-Doblas

Paperback ISBN: 978-1-5107-5856-8
Ebook ISBN: 978-1-5107-0062-8

Printed in China

Table of Contents

ACKNOWLEDGMENTS

Firstly, I would love to dedicate this book to my mother, who instilled in me the greatest work ethic and perseverance to never give up—to always have a positive attitude and to believe that anything is possible.

To my two "little cookies," as I referred to them ever since they were little, Miqueas and Mikaela, who are the loves of my life, my inspiration, and who make me better each day.

To my readers, without your support and interest in becoming a healthier you, bringing you creative, healthier recipes wouldn't be as easy. Thanks for following along.

INTRODUCTION: A BIT ABOUT ME AND MATCHA

Growing up in Spain, I was able to experience the greatest gifts this culture has to offer—especially when it came to food. Eating the Mediterranean diet and being introduced to quality ingredients and certain foods from a very young age is what molded my passion for great food as I grew older.

Since I was a child, I always loved being around the kitchen. I loved cooking and baking and always dreamed of having my own restaurant and bakery someday. Collecting cookbooks as well as recipes from cooking magazines, which I still have, was one of the things I remembered doing most when I was younger.

I also loved menu planning and going grocery shopping with my mom. Browsing the many grocery aisles and selecting ingredients to cook and bake with, talking about recipes with my older aunts, and recording new recipes I wanted to experiment with were things I enjoyed doing. Anything related to food was comforting to me.

Oftentimes as a teenager, friends and family would ask me to bake and cook for them. There was nothing that made me happier than being around food, so cooking and baking for loved ones was simply a pleasure. Since my mom worked full time while I was growing up, I was also frequently left to prepare meals for my siblings. Of course I never minded; I never considered it a chore since that is what I loved to do.

Early on, I learned and appreciated that cooking and baking from scratch using wholesome ingredients is what made food taste great and what made me feel my best. Experimenting with different flavors, textures, and ingredients is what kept me curious in the kitchen. To this date, I have never lost interest; there is nothing I enjoy more than developing healthy recipes for me and my family, and I have high hopes to be able to pass that interest and enthusiasm along to my kids.

Today, most of us know that a healthy diet plays a huge role in our well-being. When leading a healthy lifestyle, we all know that a typical balanced diet with plenty of fruit and vegetables, complex carbohydrates, healthy fats, low intake of sugars and salt, as well as consuming lean protein is most important. I believe these, coupled with having the right mindset and exercising regularly, is the secret of a good, long, quality life. Our bodies are complex machines that, without good care and the right tools, will break down and can't be used to their fullest potential.

In this cookbook, I showcase sweet and savory recipes using one of the most ancient and most powerful healthy ingredients—matcha powder. If you incorporate superfoods into your diet on a regular basis but never thought of matcha powder, now is a great time to start using it. Take advantage of the many healthy properties this ingredient has to offer!

The benefits of matcha have been well documented. Matcha is a concentrated, powerful antioxidant form of green tea that has a large number of components that are beneficial to human health. Even if you are already following a healthy lifestyle, incorporating matcha into your diet can still benefit you.

Throughout the years, I have made it a point to introduce superfoods into my cooking and baking. Since discovering matcha's potent, healthy properties, I have wanted to incorporate it into most of my meals in any way I can. Today, through this book, I can share with you some of my most valuable healthy matcha recipes, which I hope you enjoy.

History of Green Tea

Tea is a beverage with more than five thousand years of history, said to be discovered around 2500 BC. Many believe the first seeds to be imported to Japan came from Zen Monk Eisai in 1191 AD. Around that time, cultivation of tea began. Thanks to Zen Monk Eisai, matcha later become Japan's most treasured kind of green tea, as well as the tea of choice for the traditional Japanese tea ceremony. Drinking tea in Japan is much more than *just drinking tea*: the tea ceremony, called Chado, is a spiritual experience in which harmony, respect, purity, and tranquility are represented. It is a very well-respected ceremony of which Japanese people are quite proud.

Many also believed that Buddhist monks of ancient times helped tea break into the common market. Buddhist monks produced natural remedies from different plants and, since tea was known to be medicinal, it was natural for Buddhist monks to powder the green tea leaf as they would other traditional Chinese medicines. This may have been how matcha was born.

In Japanese *cha* means "tea," and *ma* means "powder," thus *matcha* translates to "powdered green tea." Because the entire leaf is ingested in powder form, it is the most potent green tea in the world. The lack of processing results in extremely high nutrient levels. Matcha is the healthiest form of tea.

Today, Japan only exports a very small amount of its production—about 4 percent of its precious matcha. Because of its great consumption in Japan, and because very little makes it out of the country, you may have to pay higher prices for this wonderful powdered tea. Matcha is not only a highly treasured specialty green tea, but it's also used frequently in Japanese cooking and baking. Because there are different grades of matcha, you must know which are best to cook and bake with.

If you want to just drink matcha and make the classic green tea, highest quality matcha is most suitable. Highest quality matchas have a higher level of antioxidants and amino acids and are more expensive. For cooking and baking, other intermediate quality varieties that are characterized by a more astringent flavor are used. These are still very good; however, the flavor as well as nutrient content may be lower.

Matcha Basics

While matcha is predominantly used for drinks such as lattes, milkshakes, and ice drinks, you can—and should—use certain grades of matcha that will work in an array of different cooking and baking recipes.

The two most popular types of matcha are Usucha, or thin tea, which creates a lighter and slightly more bitter tea, and Koicha, or thick tea, which requires significantly more matcha than Usucha to make tea. Koicha is also made with more expensive matcha and produces a milder and sweeter tea than Usucha.

Depending on the leaves used and the way of cultivating matcha, prices may vary. The matchas milled using traditional granite stone wheels, and those with deeper greener colors (as well as softest textures) tend to be more expensive and highest in quality. Making sure the tea was grown and processed in Japan is also very important when obtaining good-quality matcha, so make sure you buy from trusted sources. Matcha can also be produced in China, but Japanese matcha tends to be higher quality.

For drinks and no-bake sweet and savory recipes, use the highest quality matcha you can. The lower grades of matcha are typically more appropriate for cooking and baking. Good-quality drinking matcha powders will give you a bright green tint; however, while cooking, this tint may turn more of a distinctly yellow/brownish.

A good rule of thumb is to buy matcha powder that is tightly sealed as well as kept from light, so look for and store containers in which matcha powder cannot be seen. Once the seal is broken and the matcha is exposed to air, it will begin to oxidize. Keep it in the refrigerator to slow this process. Once matcha oxidizes, it will have a distinctive hay-like smell and a dull brownish-green color. You shouldn't wait longer than four to six weeks to consume for maximum freshness and best taste.

Buying directly from a matcha grower or a specialized supplier will ensure best quality matchas. There are many reputable online sources today, and I've listed resources at the end of this cookbook. You can buy matcha from a local tea shop or Asian grocery store but you run the risk of obtaining unfresh varieties that can produce undesired results.

When purchasing matcha, there are three different grades to consider.

Ceremonial grade is the highest grade. This type of matcha is best for drinking. It is not recommended to mix with any other foods, however, I like to use this type for most of my smoothies and drinks as well as no-bake desserts.

Premium grade is more of an everyday ingredient. It is still very good and easier to find. You can use it for both drinking and cooking.

Ingredient grade, or cooking matcha, is cheaper and is added as an ingredient to foods and beverages. Cooking matcha is blended to provide the color, aroma, and the flavor presence to withstand various processes of cooking. This grade has a stronger flavor to compete with the other flavors in foods and beverages. It is mixed with older tea leaves for this purpose.

When buying from a reputable source, the seller should be able to distinguish which matcha is better for cooking and baking and which one for just drinking. Make sure you ask questions if you are not sure the products you're considering are right for what you want to make.

Since matcha contains caffeine and it is both a stimulant and a relaxant, setting a limit to 200 milligrams is recommended. Just one cup of a matcha drink per day will allow you to feel the health benefits and improved mental alertness that matcha delivers. Doctors claim a mere 8 to 10 ounces of green tea a day is beneficial to your health.

Keep in mind that the caffeine content can vary slightly depending on the type and quality of matcha used. Koicha (thick matcha) is prepared using double the amount of matcha powder so it would have twice the caffeine. As a general rule of thumb, there are about 60 milligrams of caffeine per teaspoon of matcha; however, caffeine from matcha is absorbed into the system much slower than caffeine in coffee, as L-theanine in matcha counteracts the stimulating properties of caffeine. Compared to drinking coffee, you will experience a slower and steady release of caffeine by drinking matcha.

For perfect matcha drinks, follow these simple tips:

1. Store matcha powder in the fridge or freezer to keep it fresh. Before use, restore to room temperature.

2. Water should be hot but not boiling. If you have boiling water, allow it to cool a bit so your matcha will not taste bitter.

3. Bamboo tools and whisks will achieve the best results when mixing matcha.

4. If making iced tea, almond milk or creamer may be added.

Matcha Health Benefits

Matcha green tea is the highest quality powdered green tea available. After years of ongoing research, it has been concluded that green tea has a large amount of healthy attributes and several benefits for the human body. Because of this, we know that incorporating matcha powder into a healthy lifestyle can add longevity and aid in the fight against diseases.

Here's why:

Green tea contains four powerful flavonoid polyphenol compounds (antioxidants) known as *catechins*. Catechins are compounds that are unoxidized. Green tea contains about 30 percent catechins, whereas black tea contains only 4 percent of theaflavins. Both are powerful antioxidants, however, green tea is associated with more health benefits since it has more catechins.

These catechins in green tea are EC (epicatechin), ECG (epicatechin gallate), ECGC (Epigallocatechin gallate), and EGC (Epigallocatechin). Many studies have determined that matcha has 60 percent Epigallocatechin gallate. EGCG is tea's most abundant antioxidant catechin; it is one hundred times more potent than vitamin C, twenty-five times more potent than vitamin E, and may have therapeutic applications in the treatment of many disorders since it aids in the destruction of free radicals.

Even though EGCG is the focus of many scientific studies and has been associated with most of the newly discovered green tea benefits, there is also evidence that ECG is potent, as well.

We also know that matcha has about six times the amount of antioxidants of goji berries, sixty times that of spinach, and seventeen times the amount of blueberries. Catechins aren't found in any other foods.

There are many food items such as dark chocolate, green leafy vegetables, and some raw organic fruits that contain antioxidants; however, matcha has the highest level of antioxidant content compared to all of these foods.

Antioxidants help you fight disease and add to your longevity because they work against free radicals in the body. *Free radicals* are damaged cells that are unstable and can be problematic because they are missing a critical molecule. These free radicals often injure cells and damage DNA, which in turn can create disease by initiating mutations and uncontrolled cell growth, sometimes causing cancer.

Antioxidants are involved in the prevention of cellular damage; they block the process by neutralizing these free radicals. In doing so, the antioxidants themselves become oxidized. That is why there is a constant need to replenish our antioxidant resources and why antioxidants are so crucial to our health. Antioxidants will help you against aging, but most importantly, they will help you fight disease.

While there are several types of green tea in the market today, matcha powder is the one specially design for cooking purposes. Because matcha is ground into a fine powder, you end up ingesting the entire leaf. It is the only tea leaf in the world that can be consumed in its entirety. This process allows you to obtain all of the polyphenols and health benefits of matcha.

As a rule, the lighter the green matcha varieties, the sweeter the taste, and the darker matcha the varieties, the more astringent they are. Matcha can be used both in savory cooking and in desserts. It is a very versatile ingredient that can even be incorporated without cooking it. In this cookbook, you will find both savory and sweet dishes that will help you incorporate this ancient, powerful ingredient into your diet.

Some top health benefits of consuming matcha green tea powder are:

1. It is packed with antioxidants

Out of all the antioxidants, EGCG is the most widely recognized for its cancer-fighting properties. Scientists have found that matcha green tea contains over one hundred times more EGCG than any other tea on the market. As a result, this is the most potent cancer-fighting ingredient in the market today. As mentioned before, EGCG and other catechins counteract the effects of free radicals and disease-causing agents from the likes of pollution, UV rays, radiation, and chemicals, which can lead to cell and DNA damage, causing mutations.

2. Fights against viruses and bacteria

The catechins in matcha green tea have been shown to have antibiotic properties. Green tea may keep the immune system prepared to fend off attacks from bacteria and other pathogens, which promotes overall health. In other words, it helps you enhance your immunity.

As I mentioned, matcha tea contains epigallocatechin gallate (EGCG), which is also effective in fighting against various bacterial, viral, and fungal infections. Through research, it has been suggested that EGCG binds to the lipid membrane and exerts inhibitory action against growth of various human pathogens such as influenza A virus, hepatitis B and C virus, herpes virus, adenovirus Staphylococcus aureus bacteria, and Candida albicans yeast. More research has also proposed that the nutrients in matcha may have the ability to inhibit the attacks of HIV on human T-cells.

3.   Boosts metabolism and burns calories

Matcha powder has been found to be an energy booster that improves physical endurance in athletes. It goes as far as helping speed recovery in athletes who focus in high-intensity workouts as well as showing reverse cellular damage. Because matcha powder contains one of the highest level of catechins, there is reason to assume that consuming matcha regularly can greatly aid in workout recovery as well as encourage strength at a cellular level.

Matcha is also known for its properties in boosting the metabolism and burning fat. Research has found that consuming green tea increases thermogenesis (the body's rate of burning calories). Matcha green tea can enhance both resting metabolic rate (amount of calories burned at rest) and fat burning.

4.   Creates a sense of calm

L-theanine it is also another component of matcha green tea powder. L-theanine is an amino acid with psychoactive properties, capable of inducing alpha wave activity in the brain, which induces relaxation without the inherent drowsiness or nervous energy caused by other downers such as coffee.

5.   May lower cholesterol and blood sugar

Matcha powder is known for lowering bad cholesterol (LDL cholesterol) as well as improve insulin sensitivity in type-2 diabetes. Green tea polyphenols and polysaccharides are the components that are effective in lowering blood sugar. Polysaccharides in green tea possess the same ability to regulate blood sugar as insulin does.

If you are looking to lower your cholesterol, you should drink green tea in combination with avoiding high-cholesterol foods. While matcha powder is in no way a magic bullet, in combination with healthy lifestyle choices, this powerful ingredient can aid in lowering cholesterol as well as sugar.

6. Powerful detoxifier

Matcha is also a powerful detoxifier. Because matcha is grown in the shade, it is richer in chlorophyll than any other green tea. This chlorophyll content aids in the ability to clear the body of toxins and heavy metals, such as aluminum, lead, mercury, poisons, dioxins, and hormone disrupters. Matcha is a superior daily detox that de-acidifies the body, restores its natural pH balance, and cleans and purifies the blood.

7. Other health benefits

In addition to providing exceptional amounts of high antioxidant compounds such as catechins and polyphenols, matcha is also rich in vitamins (A, B-complex, C, E, and K). Matcha contains minerals such as manganese, potassium, calcium, and phosphorous, which are biological regulators. In addition, it is also rich in insoluble fiber and has practically no calories.

Ingredients to Use with Matcha

While eating healthy can be easier than you think, it always requires *some* planning. There are many different trends and opinions as to what is considered "eating healthy." My philosophy has always being obtaining the highest quality ingredients as well as always cooking from scratch. It has always been a lifestyle choice of mine—I need to eat healthy to be able to feel my best. Cooking and baking myself allows me to control 100 percent what I feed myself and my family. Having control of my nutrition is what makes me happy.

Cooking and baking healthy also requires having a well-stocked pantry. While some people may complain of healthy food being expensive, there is no greater expense than the cost of healthcare. The way I look at it—by investing in good-quality ingredients up front, for the most part, you'll prevent spending money later on doctors' visits, co-pays, medication, and surgery deductibles. If you think food is more expensive, think again. There is no greater expense in the United States today than the growing population of ill people.

My ingredient list includes pantry essentials that I commonly use in my kitchen. These are ingredients I use mostly on a day-to-day basis.

Organic Items

In my professional and personal opinion, there is no question that organic is best when it comes to certain food products and items such as dairy, meat, poultry, and certain fruits and vegetables. Back in the day when there were no GMO products in the market, different strains of fertilizers, and a different array of chemicals lingering in our food supply, I probably wouldn't have cared to buy organic; however, today is a different story.

There are several food items that I always buy organic that are non-negotiable in my kitchen. While these items can cost more money, the difference between organic and non-organic counterparts is most times not as much as you may think. Thanks to the high demands of organic products today, prices have decreased a lot in recent years. However, if you cannot afford buying organic products, purchasing in-season produce will ensure fewer chemicals and pesticides in these foods.

Be aware that out-of-season foods are now available year-round, flown and driven from miles away where harmful chemicals are used to keep these foods intact. Many products like hormones, antibiotics, and many other chemical substances are utilized to grow cattle quickly—a grass-fed cow will take two and a half years to grow compared to fourteen months. So you ask, should I use organic or grass-feed beef for some items? You bet!

The following are the famous dirty dozen—those fruits and vegetables that are most contaminated and should be avoided unless organic. (I also buy all of my berries organic.) If you want to start buying organic produce, start by choosing some of these items—or all of them if you can afford it.

Dirty Dozen

Peaches	Cherries
Apples	Pears
Sweet bell peppers	Grapes (imported)
Celery	Spinach
Nectarines	Lettuce
Strawberries	Potatoes

Don't waste your money on organic for the least contaminated (unless you want to!). These are:

Onions	Sweet Peas (frozen)
Avocado	Kiwi
Sweet Corn (frozen)	Bananas
Pineapples	Cabbage
Mango	Broccoli
Asparagus	

Most of my dairy such as milk, yogurt, heavy cream, butter, and cream cheese are also organic. I buy poultry that is organic and beef that is organic and/or grass feed.

Because organic products are becoming readily available, they are also beginning to become more affordable. There is no need to buy everything organic—just stick to the first list (above) and do what you can. In-season produce is best, so if you can't afford organic food, start there.

Oils

Coconut oil

Coconut oil is considered one of the superfoods of the twentieth century. While the concentration of saturated fat is high, the combination of these fatty acids is unique. Coconut oil contains medium chain triglycerides (MCTs), which are fatty acids of medium length rather than long.

Most saturated fatty acids in the diet are made of long-chain fatty acids; however, medium-chain fatty acids in coconut oil are metabolized differently and, because of this, why coconut oil has been found to have many therapeutic effects.

It can kill bacteria, viruses, and fungi, helping to stave off infections, all in part is due to its high content of Lauric acid. Coconut fatty acids are able to turn into ketones, which can help prevent seizures as well as improve brain function, especially for those suffering from Alzheimer's disease.

Coconut oil's medicinal properties have been well-documented. It is one of my favorite oils to bake with and use for no-bake desserts. I always make sure that I buy organic types and that I find virgin and unrefined varieties. Buying coconut oil in bulk is best, so if you have the opportunity to do so, you will save quite a bit of money that way.

Coconut Oil

Olive Oil

Sesame Oil

Olive oil

Olive oil, as well as extra-virgin olive oil, are my favorite oils to cook with, especially when it comes to stir-frying, sautéing, and roasting. Extra-virgin olive oil has a nuttier, stronger flavor than regular oil does since it is the most pure and least acidic. Because of this, I reserve extra-virgin olive oil to be used for salads, spreads, and such. Extra-virgin olive oil has a low smoke point, thus it is good for cold dishes and recipes that don't require heat. Also, when purchasing extra-virgin olive oil, cold press varieties are best. This ensures that its chemistry through the heat extraction process remains intact, making it a far superior type.

Whenever there is heat involved, regular olive oil is a much more stable oil than extra-virgin olive oil, thus it is my first choice when it comes to sautéing, stir-frying, and roasting.

Sesame oil

In this cookbook, you will see some Asian-inspired recipes where sesame oil is used. It is great on salad dressings and marinades. This oil has a very rich sesame taste that works very well as a flavor enhancer. When you buy sesame oil, you can store it in your cupboard; however, if you feel it is going to last you a long time, keeping it in the refrigerator will increase its shelf life. Also, something to note about sesame oil is that because it has a high smoking point, it is the least likely of the oils to go rancid.

I love using sesame oil for a simple salad dressing, which is what I use in salads most of time. I mix rice wine vinegar with sesame oil. The ratio is 2:1, using more rice wine vinegar than sesame oil. It is my favorite salad dressing. When purchasing rice wine vinegar, just make sure the sweetness doesn't come from high fructose corn syrup.

Flours and more

Gluten-free flour

I love using gluten-free flours, as I bake a lot of gluten-free recipes. I despise any store-bought gluten-free mixes because most have tons of ingredients and some of these ingredients I never use. Also, most of the gluten-free mixes are quite expensive and making your own gluten-free mix is way more economical and very easy. The gluten-free mixes I have made in the past consist of only two different types of gluten-free flour: a combination of any two from almond flour, coconut flour, oat flour, or brown rice flour.

With the following gluten-free flours, I haven't noticed much of a change in consistency when it comes to baking. Not all gluten-free flours are suitable for every dessert recipe, but with a little bit of experimentation, you will be able to learn which one works best.

My favorite gluten-free flours are:

Brown Rice Flour

I mostly use this flour when baking gluten-free cookies, pancakes, or waffles. Sometimes, I mix it with oat flour, but for the most part I try to keep the batter mixture strictly with just brown rice flour. While you can also purchase just plain rice flour, I prefer organic brown rice flour. When storing brown rice flour, make sure after you open the package you store the flour in the refrigerator.

Coconut Flour

Coconut flour is another flour that I use very often. I use this type of flour for baking recipes such as cake, muffins, cupcakes,

Oat Flour

Quinoa Flour

Brown Rice Flour

Coconut Flour

Almond Flour

or loaf breads. It is not a flour that I use in cookie recipes because I don't find coconut flour gives the conventional cookie-crunchy texture. I have seen coconut flour used in raw desserts; however, I have never tried that before. I have found coconut flour to be one of the trickiest flours to experiment with just because it behaves differently than any other flours. Coconut flour needs lots of fluid since it absorbs a lot of liquid. When baking with coconut flour most recipes call for more eggs, milk, or any other liquid of some sort. Don't be afraid of this flour. While there may be more liquid required when using this type of flour, the texture and taste are excellent for some baking desserts, especially cakes, cupcakes, and muffins.

Almond Flour

I truly love almond flour; however, because it is so expensive, I normally mix it with other gluten-free flours, especially coconut flour. I love using it for cakes, muffins, and cupcakes. This flour is also suitable for cookies and such. Even though the cookie texture may not be as crunchy, it is a great choice when it comes to baking cookie recipes. I have also used it in many raw desserts.

Buying in bulk makes this item more economical. If you buy almond flour, make sure you keep in the fridge.

Oat Flour

Oat flour is another of my favorite gluten-free flours to use because it is very easy to make. All you need to do is place gluten-free rolled oats in your food processor and pulse for a few seconds to obtain a powder/flour consistency. I have used it in cake butters, raw desserts, and pancakes. I haven't experimented with it too much at this point, but so far, so good!

Quinoa Flour

While I haven't experimented with quinoa flour that much, either, I have found it to be great in baking recipes such as cakes and cookies. You can substitute quinoa flour at about a 1:1 ratio for wheat flour. Making your own quinoa flour is also very easy. Start by rinsing the quinoa, draining, and baking for 12–15 minutes at 350 degrees Fahrenheit in a preheated oven. Then, when the quinoa is nice and dried, use a spice grinder until it is evenly ground into a flour-like consistency.

Regular Flours

Whole Wheat Pastry Flour

I have been using whole wheat pastry flour for as long as I can remember. It is my go-to regular flour for almost anything—you can use this type of flour for any baking or savory recipes from pizzas to bread to cookies, cakes, muffins, and much more. This is the reason why I started using more gluten-free flours. I was using so much whole wheat pastry flour that I wanted to change things up a bit and experiment with other options. I still love using whole wheat pastry flour; I just do it a lot less these days!

Aluminum-free Baking Soda and Aluminum-free Baking Powder

Not long ago, I made the switch to aluminum-free baking soda and baking powder. It is surprising to see how many different chemicals the food industry introduces to some of our food items that are actually not required. If you haven't tried aluminum-free baking soda or baking powder, I suggest you do so. They are not much more expensive and they're better for you.

Why on Earth would you want aluminum in your baking recipes? I sure don't.

Arrowroot Powder

I use this powder in place of corn starch. It actually behaves in the same manner as corn starch, as it is also a thickener; however, arrowroot powder is a healthier option. The process of making arrowroot powder is far better than how corn starch is made. I won't get into the nitty gritty, but if you can get your hands on arrowroot powder instead of corn starch, I greatly suggest switching to this healthier ingredient.

Grains

Quinoa

I love using organic quinoa. I always buy it in bulk because it can get very expensive. I normally use quinoa interchangeably with organic brown rice. Just make sure when using quinoa that you rinse it a few times prior to using. Also, store quinoa in a cool, dry place properly sealed either in its original package or in a glass container with an hermetic seal. You can also make your own quinoa flour to use in your baking recipes, so instead of wasting money, just invest a few minutes to make your own.

Organic Brown Rice

Brown rice is one of the grains we eat most in my house. I didn't want my kids to get bored of rice, so I started using quinoa and changing things a bit. Don't get me wrong—I do love to eat brown rice, but I find having a variety of ingredients works best, especially when it comes to feeding kids. Just make sure you buy organic brown rice varieties as well as use brown rice varieties that have more minerals, vitamins, and fiber than the regular white rice kinds.

Whole Wheat Pasta

Like whole wheat pastry flour, I found myself using a lot of whole wheat pasta. I do love pasta, and pasta recipes are very common on my weekly menus. For this reason, I also started using gluten-free pasta. As a rule of thumb, we never use any white grains such as white flours, white pasta,

white rice, or white bread. I always buy 100 percent whole wheat grains. Complex carbohydrates are the sources of 100 percent whole grains, so I suggest purchasing these rather than the white varieties for a healthier option.

Gluten Free Pasta

Quinoa

Rolled Oats

Whole Wheat Pasta

Brown Rice

Gluten-Free Pasta

Though a little bit more expensive, I like to use a gluten-free variety of pasta from time to time. As stated, I cook so much pasta during the week that I switched to gluten-free pastas and found it to be beneficial. The types that I enjoy most are those that mix a couple of gluten-free flours such as quinoa and brown rice flour.

Rolled Oats

Rolled oats is another very common food staple in my house. I also buy this in bulk; however, buying gluten-free rolled oats can be a little bit trickier for those that need them. I have found gluten-free rolled oats in smaller packages; however, since none of my family members are celiac, spending the extra money is not necessary for us. If you are celiac, however, buying gluten-free rolled oats is a must.

Nuts and Seeds

While nuts and seeds may be high in calories and fats, these fats are not only the healthier ones, but the array of good nutrients nuts and seeds provide outweighs the high caloric content. In moderation, nuts and seeds are a nutrient-dense food source of many essential minerals, vitamins, and protein, so don't be afraid to cook and bake with these. I normally choose raw varieties and modify them according to the recipe. If they need to be toasted, baked, or salted, I like to be the one to control that. When storing nuts and seeds, I always use glass containers with hermetic lids. If you are keeping nuts for a long time, I suggest freezing them. Because they are high in oil, if you keep nuts outside for too long, they may become rancid.

Some of my favorite nuts and seeds to cook with follow; however, on occasion I also enjoy brazil nuts and hazelnuts.

Cashews

Cashew nuts are packed with energy, antioxidants, minerals, and vitamins essential for our health. They have a ton of soluble dietary fiber, vitamins, minerals, and numerous health-promoting phyto-chemicals that help protect us from diseases and cancers. Cashews are a great nut, especially while making vegan dessert recipes. It is one of the nuts I rely most on, as I can use it to make vegan ice cream with a creamier consistency or for energy bars, crusts, and much more.

Sunflower Seeds

Sesame Seeds

Pistachios

Almonds

Walnuts

Pumpkin Seeds

Cashews

Almonds

Almonds are another nutrient power house because they lower cholesterol, help to build strong bones and teeth, and are also high in protein. They have an array of benefits and are very versatile for many recipes. For the most part, I like to consume almonds in their raw state or use in crusts for raw desserts and when making nut butter. In addition, on occasion I like to bake with almond flour when making gluten-free cakes and muffins. Almonds can also be great in trail mixes and granola.

Walnuts

Walnuts are the nuts I grew up eating. My relatives had walnut trees and we always ate them as a snack. Like almonds, I like to enjoy walnuts in their raw state; however, this is the nut that I tend to also like lightly roasted and added to salads. Like almonds, walnuts are great for heart health and cancer-fighting properties. They contain antioxidants and omega-3 fatty acids and help to reduce inflammation.

Pistachios

Pistachios are my kids' favorite nut. Like many other nuts, pistachios are great for heart health because they contain L-arginine, which can make the lining of your arteries more flexible and decrease the likelihood of developing blood clots that could cause a heart attack. They are also rich in vitamin E, which makes it less likely for your arteries to become clogged with plaque. Pistachios, like any other nuts, are great sprinkled in salads, yogurt, granola, trail mixes, and even added to smoothies to increase protein content.

Pumpkin Seeds

Pumpkin seeds are very rich in zinc, which is important for immunity, sleep, mood, eye, and skin health, insulin regulation, and male sexual function. Pumpkin seeds are rich in tryptophan, an amino acid the body converts into serotonin, which in turn is converted into melatonin, the sleep hormone, thus it may help you sleep better. Roasted pumpkin seeds are great and are an awesome snack to keep around.

Sesame Seeds

I love using sesame seeds for salad and Asian cooking. Its rich flavor is intoxicating and, while I use black sesame seeds more often for their higher mineral content, I do use white sesame seeds together with black for the contrast in color. Sesame seeds are high in copper, manganese, and calcium, and they are also good for digestion. Like pumpkin seeds, sesame also contain thiamin and tryptophan that help produce serotonin, which reduces pain, assists in regulating moods, and helps you sleep deeply.

Sunflower Seeds

Sunflower seeds are a rich source of vitamins E and B-1, as well as copper. Sunflower seeds are one of the most predominant seeds in Spain. I love adding these seeds to salads and even eating them raw. They are a great snack to have around since they can be added to an array of dishes.

Beans and Legumes

Even though I am not strictly vegetarian anymore, I was for eighteen years. I relied on beans and legumes because they are an excellent source of protein and fiber. They also have vitamins and minerals and are nutrient dense. Lentils and garbanzo beans, or the so-called chickpeas, are the ones I use most. I love lentils because they are high in iron, they cook really fast, and you can find them in an array of colors. They are a great ingredient to add to your salads, soups, and stews and are a good alternative to meat. I have used chickpeas in both savory and sweet recipes. I love how versatile they are and, like lentils, they are very rich in iron. On occasion, I also use black and red beans. These are great in soups and stews, and I have also used them to bake cakes with. Puréed, they are a healthy alternative ingredient for cake batters. Like with nuts and seeds, whenever possible I like to store my beans and legumes in glass containers.

Sweeteners

Maple syrup, medjool dates, honey, and coconut sugar are my healthier sweeteners of choice while baking and sometimes cooking.

Honey

While I don't use honey that much for baking (its properties get degraded with heat), occasionally I like to add it to smoothies, toasts, and things of that nature. I also like to buy raw varieties, as the flavor and nutrient quality is superior than conventional honey brands.

Coconut Sugar

I have recently switched to using coconut sugar, also called coconut palm sugar, for most of my baking. Coconut sugar is rich in certain minerals such as iron, zinc, calcium, and potassium. It contains a fiber called Inulin, which may slow glucose absorption and is why coconut sugar has a lower glycemic index than regular table sugar. Coconut sugar is a great healthier alternative to use in place of white sugar, so I highly recommended switching to this type.

Maple Syrup

I probably use maple syrup more often than any other type of sweetener. Maple syrup is actually made from the sugary circulating fluid (sap) of maple trees. The fluid is collected and boiled to remove impurities to make it a thicker, more concentrated syrup.

CoconutSugar

Maple Syrup

Dates

Raw Honey

on what you are making, you can choose from the following: Light Amber, Medium Amber, and Dark Amber (all Grade A) and then a darker type (Grade B).

The main difference between them is that the darker syrups are made from sap extracted later in the harvesting season. The dark syrups have a stronger maple flavor and are typically used for baking, while the lighter ones are used directly as syrups like on pancakes.

Medjool Dates

Medjool dates are a good source of fiber and contain high levels of essential minerals like potassium, magnesium, copper, and manganese. Most contain a significant amount of fruit sugar, but this can make them a good alternative to more caloric desserts.

While you can use Medjool dates in regular meat dishes and baked goods, I normally use these when making raw desserts. Turning them into a paste and

I tend to use this sweetener for both raw and baking desserts. There are different types of maple syrups you can use and, depending

combining them with nuts makes a great starter batter that can later be altered to suit your needs. I use this starter batter for energy bites, protein bars, and much more. When purchasing dates, since I use them a lot, I mostly store them in my pantry; however, if you buy them in bulk and you suspect they will last you a long time, storing them in the fridge will make them last for at least three months.

Other Superfoods

While I use many other dried fruits (making sure they are free of sulfur dioxide) and superfoods not mentioned in this list, these are the ones that I constantly keep in my pantry at all times.

Chia Seeds

Chia seeds are a nutrient power house. Not only are they a great source of omega-3 fatty acids, which have anti-inflammatory properties, but they are also an excellent source of fiber, amino acids, minerals, and antioxidants.

Chia seeds are great in an array of recipes; however, cooking or baking these seeds will interfere with their many nutritional properties, so these are best consumed while they are in their raw state. There are a few recipes in this cookbook using chia seeds, but you can also add them to yogurts, smoothies, drinks, and frozen pops.

Flaxseed Meal

Flaxseed meal is another rich nutrient power house. I like to use the meal and not the seeds because the nutrients reside inside the seed. Like chia seeds, flaxseed meal is very rich in omega-3 fatty acids and is an excellent source of fiber, especially soluble fiber, which aids in lowering cholesterol.

Flaxseed meal can be added to smoothies, yogurts, cereal, and is actually used for vegan baking in place of regular eggs. Flax eggs are made by mixing one tablespoon of ground flaxseed meal and three tablespoons of water.

Goji Berries

Goji berries have several health benefits because of their nutrient-rich content. They are said to benefit mental well-being and calmness, athletic performance, happiness, and quality of sleep. They are another ingredient said to contain the most vitamins,

Hulled Hemp Seeds

Dried Hemp Seeds

Cacao Nibs

Chia Seeds

Flaxseed Meal

cooked, steamed, and processed in any way after they are washed.

Hemp Seeds

I love hemp seeds. Hemp seeds provide a healthy dose of protein, omega-3 fatty acids, fiber, antioxidants, and minerals.

Lately, I have been using two different kinds—hulled hemp seeds and the conventional hemp seed. Their light flavor allows them to blend easily into desserts, granola, cereal, yogurt, and other types of savory recipes such as salads, rice dishes, and pilafs. Because of their high oil content, hemp seeds should be stored in an airtight container in the fridge or freezer to keep fresh.

Spices and Condiments

Besides my nut collection, my spice pantry section is one of the most abundant in my kitchen. I love cooking with a variety of spices since I love to cook different types of cuisines. My favorite cuisines are Indian, Thai, Spanish, Moroccan, and the list goes on.

minerals, and antioxidants as well as fiber. Goji berries can be added to trail mixes, smoothies, granola, or as a garnish on cereals, salads, or yogurts. Goji berries can be baked,

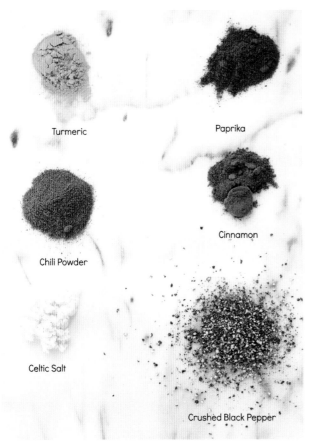

Turmeric

Paprika

Chili Powder

Cinnamon

Celtic Salt

Crushed Black Pepper

I will not give you the extensive list of spices I have in my pantry, but the ones I use most are cinnamon, turmeric, Spanish paprika, red chili, and black pepper.

Celtic Salt

When I use salt, Celtic salt is my choice for the simple reason that it is unrefined and its nutrient content, especially mineral content, has not been tampered with. Because Celtic salt is unrefined and naturally occurring, essential minerals are still intact. There also no additives on this type of salt. I have used both light grey and fine ground varieties, however, I prefer light gray because it is 100 percent natural.

MATCHA RECIPES

ENERGIZING BREAKFASTS

GRANOLA

gluten-free | heart-healthy | vegetarian

Yield: 12-14 servings

4 cups rolled oats
½ cup maple syrup
1 cup walnut pieces
¼ coconut oil, melted
1 teaspoon matcha powder

1 cup dried cranberries
⅓ cup dark chocolate chips
¼ cup goji berries
⅓ cup chia seeds

Preheat oven to 275 degrees Fahrenheit.

In a large mixing bowl, mix rolled oats, maple syrup, walnuts, coconut oil, and matcha powder. Spread mixture on a 9 x 13 square baking pan. Bake for 20 minutes.

Remove baking pan from the oven and stir mixture with a spatula. Bake for another 20 minutes, repeating this step once more until the granola is golden and crisp.

Transfer the granola to a large mixing bowl. Add the dried cranberries, dark chocolate chips, goji berries, and chia seeds. Mix thoroughly. Let the granola cool completely. Serve as desired with milk, yogurt, or any other mix-ins of your choice.

Store granola in an airtight container for up to 1 month.

Miryam's Note: Use gluten-free rolled oats for a gluten-free version. You can also add any other nuts and dried fruit of your choice.

MANGO PROTEIN SMOOTHIE

gluten-free | dairy-free | heart-healthy | low-fat | vegetarian | vegan

Yield: 4 servings

3 cups almond milk
2 cups frozen mango chunks
2 scoops vanilla hemp protein powder
1 teaspoon matcha powder

In a blender, add all the ingredients and pulse until you obtain a homogenous mixture. Depending on the blender, this should take about 30 seconds.

Serve immediately.

Miryam's Note: You can also use fresh mango and ice to thicken the mixture.

OVERNIGHT OATS

gluten-free | low-fat | dairy-free | vegetarian | vegan

Yield: 10–12 servings

6 cups almond milk
4 cups rolled oats
¼ cup maple syrup
¼ cup chia seeds
¼ cup unsweetened shredded coconut
¼ cup pumpkin seeds
1 teaspoon matcha powder

In a large mixing bowl, add all the ingredients and mix thoroughly. If you noticed the mixture is too dry, add more milk, as the rolled oats and chia seeds will absorb some of the milk overnight.

Place mixture in the refrigerator overnight. Serve the next morning with some extra nuts and milk, if desired.

Miryam's Note: You can serve these oats cold or warm. I like mine lukewarm so I warm my serving for about a minute in the microwave. I also tend to add some unsweetened coconut chips for some crunch.

BREAKFAST SMOOTHIE BOWL

gluten-free | dairy-free | heart-healthy | vegetarian | vegan

Yield: 3 servings

4 frozen bananas
⅓ cup almond milk
½ teaspoon chlorella
1 teaspoon matcha powder

Topping
½ banana, sliced
1 tablespoon chia seeds
2 tablespoons unsweetened shredded coconut

In a blender or food processor, add bananas, almond milk, chlorella, and matcha powder. Pulse until the mixture is homogenous, about 30 seconds depending on the power of your machine. Transfer mixture to a bowl and top with topping ingredients.

Serve immediately.

Miryam's Note: You can also add moringa powder in place of chlorella or some extra matcha powder if none of these two ingredients are available to you. You can also sprinkle some goji berries for some extra health benefits, such as increasing your quality of sleep and improving your mental well-being.

BREAKFAST FRITTATA

gluten-free | vegetarian | nut-free

Yield: 6 servings

2 tablespoons olive oil
32 ounces egg whites
2 whole organic eggs
1 teaspoon matcha powder
1 teaspoon turmeric powder

½ teaspoon Celtic salt
½ teaspoon ground pepper
1 cup fresh kale
5 ounces goat cheese
2 ounces sundried tomatoes in oil, drained

Preheat your oven to 425 degrees Fahrenheit

Grease a 12-inch cast-iron skillet, or any other large skillet, with 1 tablespoon of olive oil. Set aside.

In a large mixing bowl, add the egg whites, whole eggs, the remainder of the olive oil, matcha powder, turmeric powder, salt, and pepper. Whisk to combine the ingredients. Place the egg mixture in the prepared cast-iron skillet and sprinkle the kale, crumbled goat cheese, and sundried tomatoes over the egg mixture.

Bake it in the preheated oven for 25–30 minutes or until the top starts to bubble and it appears cooked. Turn the heat off and let it sit in the oven for 5 minutes.

Serve frittata while still warm with some whole-grain bread.

Miryam's Note: You can place under the broiler for 1–2 minutes on high to brown the top of the frittata.

CREAM CHEESE SPREAD

vegetarian

Yield: 8 servings

8 ounces cream cheese, room temperature
2 teaspoons matcha powder
3 tablespoons honey
4 whole-grain bagels, sliced

Topping
1 tablespoon chia seeds
¼ cup pumpkin seeds

In a small mixing bowl, add the cream cheese, matcha powder, and honey. With a handheld electric mixer or stand-up mixer, mix the ingredients until you obtain a homogenous spread.

Spread the cream cheese mixture over each bagel slice and sprinkle with some chia and pumpkin seeds.

Serve immediately.

Miryam's Note: Store leftover cream cheese spread in a glass container in the refrigerator for up to 2 weeks. For a gluten-free version, use gluten-free bagels.

KIWI PINEAPPLE CHIA JAM

gluten-free | dairy-free | heart-healthy | vegetarian | nut-free | vegan

Yield: 1½ cups

4 kiwis, peeled and cut into chunks
⅓ cup pineapple, chopped
3 tablespoons maple syrup
3 tablespoons chia seeds
1 teaspoon matcha powder

Add the kiwis, pineapple, and maple syrup in a blender or food processor and pulse until puréed. Add the mixture to a medium bowl. Add the chia seeds and matcha powder. Combine mixture with a spatula or spoon until the seeds are well incorporated.

Transfer mixture to an 8-ounce mason jar and store in the fridge for 2–3 hours until the mixture thickens.

You can use this jam over toast or with your peanut butter sandwich, yogurt, or ice cream.

Miryam's Note: You can experiment with this recipe and use any other puréed fruit of your choice. If you don't like kiwis, raspberries and strawberries work very well.

NO-BAKE BREAKFAST BARS

gluten-free | heart-healthy | vegetarian

Yields: 6 bars

2 cups rolled oats
¾ cup cashew nuts
½ cup pitted dates
¼ cup chia seeds

2 tablespoons coconut oil, melted
1 tablespoon almond milk
2 teaspoons matcha powder
3 ounces dark chocolate chips

Line a 9 x 5-inch loaf pan with unbleached parchment paper and set aside.

Add all the ingredients, except chocolate chips, in a food processor and pulse until the mixture comes together.

Transfer mixture to the prepared baking pan and press down with a spatula, making sure it is uniform on all sides. Place bars in the fridge for at least 3–4 hours to harden.

In the meantime, place chocolate chips in a microwave-safe bowl. Melt in the microwave in 15- to 30-second intervals, stirring in between until completely melted.

Take the bars out of the fridge and lift the parchment paper with the bars off the baking pan. Cut into bars and drizzle with the melted chocolate.

Store leftover bars in the refrigerator, covered.

Miryam's Note: For a vegan version, use dairy-free chocolate chips.

BREAKFAST MUFFINS

Yield: 12 regular-sized muffins

1 egg
1 cup Greek yogurt
½ cup unrefined sugar
⅓ cup almond milk
2 teaspoons vanilla extract
¼ cup olive oil
1 cup whole wheat pastry flour

⅓ cup walnuts, chopped
⅓ cup golden raisins
¾ cup rolled oats
1 teaspoon cinnamon powder
3 teaspoons baking powder
1 teaspoon matcha powder
¼ teaspoon Celtic salt

Preheat oven to 350 degrees Fahrenheit. Line a 12-cup regular muffin pan with cupcake liners and set aside.

In a large mixing bowl, add the egg, Greek yogurt, sugar, almond milk, vanilla extract, and olive oil. With a whisk or electric mixer, combine until the ingredients come together. Add the rest of the ingredients to the mixing bowl and, with a spatula, combine until the batter is smooth and homogenous and all the ingredients are well mixed in.

With a medium cookie scoop, fill each cupcake liner ¾ full. Bake for 25–30 minutes or until a tester inserted in the middle of each muffin comes out clean. Remove baking pan from the oven and muffins from the pan. Cool muffins on a cooling rack until completely cool.

Store muffins in a closed glass container or cake stand in the kitchen counter for up to 3–5 days.

Alternatively, you can individually freeze the muffins and eat as you'd like.

BREAKFAST PARFAITS

Yield: 4 parfaits

2 cups plain Greek yogurt
2 tablespoon maple syrup
1 tablespoon matcha powder
2 cups low-sugar granola
1 cup fresh mixed berries

In a medium mixing bowl, mix the plain Greek yogurt, maple syrup, and matcha powder.

In four serving glasses, add 2–3 tablespoons Greek yogurt mixture to the bottom of each glass. Top with ¼ cup granola. Add some mixed berries over the granola and repeat layers, ending with the yogurt mixture and more mixed berries.

Serve immediately. You can store parfaits for up to 1 day in the refrigerator.

Miryam's Note: You can use any other chopped fresh fruit of your choice.

ENERGY TRUFFLES

gluten-free | vegan | vegetarian | dairy-free |
heart-healthy

Yield: 24 medium truffles

Truffles
2 cups pitted dates
1 cup almond flour
¼ cup chia seeds
¼ cup flaxseed meal
¼ cup cocoa powder
¼ cup maple syrup
1 teaspoon matcha powder
2 tablespoons almond milk or water

Coating
1–2 tablespoons cocoa powder
1–2 tablespoons chia seeds
1–2 tablespoons almond flour
1–2 tablespoons unsweetened
    shredded coconut

Place the truffle ingredients in your food processor and pulse until the mixture comes together. If you find the mixture still doesn't come together, add 1 extra tablespoon of almond milk or water. Transfer the mixture to a small bowl.

With your hands, roll the mixture into small balls and coat them with either almond flour, cacao powder, chia seeds, or shredded coconut.

Store in an airtight container in the refrigerator for up to 5 days. Alternatively, you can freeze the truffles in a BPA-free zip top bag and eat as you'd like.

'NANA ICE CREAM

gluten-free | vegan | heart-healthy | vegetarian | dairy-free | nut-free

Yield: 4 servings

3 frozen bananas
½ cup fresh spinach
⅓ cup almond milk
1 teaspoon matcha powder

Place all ingredients in your food processor or blender and pulse until it comes together.

Serve immediately with your favorite toppings.

Miryam's Note: You can use any topping of your choice. I used raw cacao nibs and sweetened shredded coconut. I sometimes add nut butter, like almond or peanut butter, to the 'nana ice cream mix. It's delicious.

ENERGY BARS

gluten-free | vegan | vegetarian | dairy-free

Yield: 12–18 bars

1 cup pitted dates
1 cup unsweetened coconut, shredded
1 cup raw pistachios
3 tablespoons chia seeds
2–3 tablespoons water
2 teaspoons matcha powder

Line an 8 x 8-inch square cake pan with unbleached parchment paper and set aside.

Add all the ingredients in a food processor and pulse until the mixture comes together.

Transfer mixture to the prepared baking pan and press down with a spatula, making sure it is uniform.

Place bars in the fridge for 3–4 hours to solidify. Take mixture out of the fridge and lift the parchment paper from the baking pan with the bars. Cut into bars or squares.

Store bars in a glass container in the refrigerator, covered.

Miryam's Note: If you don't like pistachios, you can use any other nuts of your choice.

KALE AND HOT PEPPER GRILLED CHEESE SANDWICH

vegetarian

Yield: 4 sandwiches

2 tablespoons butter, room temperature
½ teaspoon matcha powder
8 whole-grain bread slices
16 slices provolone cheese
2 ounces fresh kale
2 red hot peppers, sliced

Heat a cast-iron griddle over medium to low heat.

Mix the butter and matcha powder until they are well combined.

Spread the butter over the inside of four slices of bread. Place one slice of the provolone cheese onto each of the four slices of bread followed by fresh kale and sliced hot peppers. Place the other cheese slice on top of the kale and top with the other slice of bread.

Place sandwiches onto the hot griddle until the side turns golden brown and the cheese begins to melt, about 2–4 minutes. Turn sandwich over and grill for another 2–4 minutes, making sure the bread doesn't burn.

Miryam's Note: You can use any cheese of your choice. Swiss, gruyere, and American cheese are also great options.

ENERGIZING SMOOTHIE

gluten-free | vegan | vegetarian | dairy-free | heart-healthy

Yield: 4 servings

3 ripe frozen bananas
4 cups almond milk
2 scoops hemp protein powder
2 cups fresh organic spinach
1 tablespoon matcha powder

Place all the ingredients in a blender and blend until smooth. Serve immediately in tall glasses.

Miryam's Note: You can use this mixture and make frozen pops for a refreshing, healthy treat.

AVOCADO AND EGGS ON FLATBREAD

vegetarian | dairy-free | heart-healthy | nut-free

Yield: 4 servings

2 tablespoons olive oil
4 organic eggs
2 avocados
whole wheat flatbread
1 teaspoon matcha powder

2 teaspoons hot sauce
2 ounces pea shoots
pinch Celtic salt
pinch ground pepper

Over medium to high heat, place the olive oil in a large nonstick skillet and add the eggs. Cook until the eggs are done, about 2–3 minutes. Set aside.

Peel the avocados and mash with a fork. Divide the avocado purée between the flatbreads and sprinkle the matcha powder over the avocado. Arrange the cooked eggs over the avocado and drizzle with hot sauce. Divide the pea shoots between each slice of bread and sprinkle with salt and pepper.

Serve immediately.

Miryam's Note: You can add any other vegetables of your choice. Fresh tomatoes and green onions work really well. If you would like to keep this recipe gluten-free use gluten-free flatbread.

LEMON COCONUT BITES

gluten-free | vegetarian | vegan

Yield: 20–24 bites

1 cup rolled oats
1 cup raw cashews
½ cup pitted dates
⅓ cup unsweetened shredded coconut
1–2 lemons, juiced
1 teaspoon matcha powder
2 teaspoons lemon extract, optional

Place all the ingredients in a food processor and pulse until they come together. Roll the dough into bite-sized balls and dip into some extra unsweetened shredded coconut, if desired.

Store lemon coconut bites in the refrigerator, covered.

DARK CHOCOLATE POMEGRANATE SEED BITES

gluten-free | vegetarian | heart-healthy

Yield: 12–16 bites

6 ounces dark chocolate chips
2 ounces pomegranate seeds
¼ cup pistachios, chopped
1 teaspoon matcha powder

Line a baking sheet with unbleached parchment paper and set aside.

Place chocolate chips in a microwave-safe bowl and melt in 30-second intervals, stirring in between until melted.

Drizzle dollops of chocolate 2–3 inches apart in the prepared baking sheets, spreading each with the back of a spoon. Place a few pomegranate seeds and pistachios over the chocolate. Repeat until you use all the chocolate, pomegranate seeds, and pistachios. Sprinkle the matcha powder over each piece and set the tray aside until the chocolate sets.

Store chocolate bites on the kitchen counter.

Miryam's Note: For a dairy-free version, use dairy-free chocolate chips.

SESAME SQUARES

gluten-free | vegetarian | heart-healthy | dairy-free

Yield: 12–16 squares

2 cups pitted dates
1 cup sesame seeds
¼ cup goji berries
½ cup dried apricots
¼ cup flaxseed meal

1 cup almond flour
¼ teaspoon Celtic salt
1 teaspoon matcha powder
1 teaspoon vanilla extract

Line an 8 x 8-inch square cake pan with unbleached parchment paper and set aside.

Add all the ingredients in a food processor and pulse until the mixture comes together.

Transfer mixture to the prepared baking pan and press down with a spatula, making sure it is uniform.

Place bars in the fridge for 3–4 hours to solidify. Take mixture out of the fridge and lift the parchment paper off the baking pan. Cut into bars or squares.

Store bars in a glass container in the refrigerator, covered.

RICOTTA AND CUCUMBER TOASTS

vegetarian | heart-healthy | nut-free

Yield: 4 servings

4 whole grain bread slices
1 small cucumber
2 medium radishes
1 cup ricotta cheese

1 teaspoon matcha powder
2 ounces pea shoots
pinch ground pepper
pinch Celtic salt

Slice cucumber and radishes with a grater and set aside. Place ¼ cup ricotta cheese over each slice of bread and spread the cheese with a spoon. Sprinkle the matcha powder over each slice. Arrange the cucumber and radish slices over the ricotta and sprinkle the pea shoots.

Sprinkle with the ground pepper and salt and serve immediately.

Miryam's Note: You can use soft crumbled tofu for a vegan version and use gluten-free bread for a gluten-free option.

GREEN TEA FRAPPUCCINO

vegetarian | heart-healthy | vegan | dairy-free | gluten-free | nut-free

Yield: 4 servings

1 14-ounce can full-fat coconut milk or cream
3–4 cups ice
1 teaspoon matcha
2 tablespoons maple syrup
1 teaspoon vanilla extract

Place all ingredients in a blender and blend until smooth.

Serve immediately.

Miryam's Note: You can use any other milk of choice.

BARLEY RISOTTO

vegetarian | heart-healthy

Yield: 6 servings

3 cups barley

6–7 cups vegetable stock

20 ounces mushrooms, sliced

2 tablespoons olive oil

1 small onion, chopped

20 ounces mushrooms, sliced

4–5 garlic cloves, chopped

1 teaspoon Celtic salt

½ cup white wine

2 teaspoons matcha powder

1 teaspoon thyme powder

⅓ cup parmesan cheese

fresh thyme

In a 3-quart Dutch oven over medium to high heat, add the olive oil and onions. Cook for 2–3 minutes until translucent. Add the sliced mushrooms and cook for 3–5 minutes.

Add the garlic and salt and cook the garlic until fragrant, about one minute. Add the white wine and reduce by half. Add the barley, matcha powder, and thyme powder and coat the barley with the pan ingredients. Add 2 cups of vegetable stock and bring the mixture to a boil. Reduce the flame to low and don't add any more liquid until the vegetable stock has been consumed. Repeat this step until all your liquid is gone, adding 2 cups at a time and stirring the risotto in between adding more stock.

When the barley is soft, make sure you still have a little bit of visible vegetable stock in the pan, and turn the heat off. At this stage, you can add the herbs and parmesan cheese. Stir and serve while still warm.

Miryam's Note: If you find your barley is still hard after the 6-7 cups of vegetable stock have been absorbed, add more until your barley softens. It may take you an extra 2 cups depending on what type of barley you used. (I used Trader Joe's brand.)

FISH CURRY

gluten-free | heart-healthy | dairy-free

Yield: 6-8 servings

2 tablespoons olive oil
1 onion, chopped
1 tablespoon green curry paste
1 14-ounce can coconut cream
½ cup vegetable stock
2 tablespoons Thai fish sauce
1 teaspoon matcha powder

1 tablespoon sugar
1 tomato, cut into cubes
1½ pounds Mahi Mahi, cut into cubes
12 ounces fresh broccoli florets
1 lime, juiced
fresh cilantro, chopped

Heat oil in nonstick large skillet over medium to high heat. Add chopped onion and cook for 3 minutes or so until soft or beginning to brown.

Reduce heat to medium and add the curry paste. Stir until fragrant, about 1 minute. Add coconut cream, vegetable stock, fish sauce, matcha powder, and sugar. Bring to a boil. Add the tomatoes and Mahi Mahi. Cook further for 5 minutes or until fish is almost cooked.

Add the fresh broccoli and cook another 2–3 minutes. Add lime juice and garnish with cilantro.

Miryam's Note: Serve fish curry with some brown rice and extra lime wedges. You can also use any other firm fish of your choice (such as tile fish or halibut) as well as coconut milk in place of the coconut cream.

NOODLE SALAD WITH ASIAN VINAIGRETTE

dairy-free | vegetarian | vegan

Yield: 4 servings

10 ounces Japanese curly noodles
   (ramen or udon)
2 tablespoon olive oil
16 ounces extra-firm tofu, cut into cubes
8 radishes, thinly sliced
4 scallions, thinly sliced
1 large cucumber, thinly sliced
1 cup fresh cilantro leaves

Vinaigrette
¼ cup reduced sodium soy sauce
¼ cup rice wine vinegar
1 tablespoon unrefined sugar
1 tablespoon sesame oil
1 teaspoon matcha powder
1 teaspoon pepper flakes

Cook noodles according to package instructions. Drain and set aside.

In a medium mixing bowl, combine vinaigrette ingredients. Set aside.

In a nonstick skillet, over medium to high heat, add the olive oil. Add the cubed tofu and cook, stirring occasionally for 5–8 minutes or until browned.

To assemble the noodles, place the noodles in a large bowl followed by the sliced radishes, scallions, and cucumber. Add the cooked tofu, vinaigrette, and cilantro leaves and toss to combine.

Serve immediately.

QUINOA BURGERS WITH MATCHA HABANERO MAYO

gluten-free | vegetarian

Yield: 6 medium burgers

1 cup uncooked quinoa
1 organic egg
1 teaspoon matcha powder
⅓ cup mayonnaise
2 ounces shredded carrots, chopped
2 ounces frozen peas, thawed
1 teaspoon Celtic salt
2 tablespoon olive oil

Matcha Habanero Mayo
⅓ cup mayonnaise
2–3 tablespoons green habanero sauce
1 tablespoon water
1 teaspoon matcha powder
½ teaspoon Celtic salt

Cook quinoa according to package instructions. Once the quinoa is cooked, let it cool.

While the quinoa cools, add the mayo ingredients to a small mixing bowl and mix until combined. Set aside.

In a large mixing bowl, place the egg and beat with a fork. Add the matcha powder and mayonnaise and mix with a whisk until the powder has been dissolved. Add the chopped carrots and peas to the bowl and combine. Add the quinoa and salt to the bowl. Mix until all the ingredients are well incorporated.

Form burger patties and place on a clean plate. In a nonstick skillet, over medium to low heat, heat the olive oil. Add the burger patties and cook on each side for 4–5 minutes or until lightly browned. Serve while still warm over whole-grain buns, with the Matcha Habanero Mayo and sliced veggies of your choice.

CURRIED COCONUT BROCCOLI SOUP

dairy-free | vegetarian | gluten-free | heart-healthy

Yield: 4 servings

2 tablespoons olive oil
1 onion, chopped
3 garlic cloves, chopped
1 tablespoon green curry paste
1 14-ounce can coconut cream

1 teaspoon matcha powder
12 ounces fresh broccoli florets
1 teaspoon Celtic salt
4–5 cups water

In your 5-quart Dutch oven, or any large pot, over medium to high heat, add the olive oil and onions and cook for about 3–5 minutes or until translucent. Add the garlic and cook for 1 minute or until fragrant. Add the green curry paste followed by the coconut cream and matcha powder and cook, stirring, for another minute. Add the broccoli florets, salt, and water stir and let it cook until the broccoli is tender, about 5 minutes.

Turn the heat off. With an immersion blender, blend the soup until smooth. Serve while still warm.

Miryam's Note: You can use coconut milk in place of the coconut cream.

QUINOA STIR-FRY

dairy-free | gluten-free

Yield: 4 servings

2 tablespoons olive oil
1½ organic chicken breasts, cut into chunks
1 red organic pepper, chopped
1 orange pepper, chopped
1 onion, chopped
1 tablespoon ginger, chopped

¼ cup cashews
1 teaspoon matcha powder
2 cups cooked quinoa
⅓ cup soy sauce
2 spring onions, sliced

Place the olive oil on a large skillet over medium to high heat and add the chicken pieces. Cook for about 5 minutes. Add the chopped peppers and onion and cook for 3–5 minutes, stirring occasionally, until cooked.

Add the ginger, cashews, and matcha powder and cook for an extra minute. Add the cooked quinoa followed by the soy sauce and combine. Sprinkle the chopped spring onions and serve while still warm.

Miryam's Note: You can use any other colored peppers. I like to use a variety of colorful ones when they are in season. If you want to make this recipe vegetarian, you can use extra-firm tofu in place of chicken. For a gluten-free version, make sure you use a brand of soy sauce that is gluten free.

BAKED CHICKEN FINGERS WITH SPICY MAYO

gluten-free

Yield: 4 servings

½ cup almond flour
¼ cup mixed sesame seeds
¼ cup parmesan cheese
2 pounds chicken tenders

Spicy Mayo
½ cup mayonnaise
¼ cup fresh lemon juice
½ teaspoon matcha powder
1 teaspoon garlic salt
½ teaspoon ground black pepper

Preheat the oven to 375 degrees Fahrenheit. Line a baking sheet with unbleached parchment paper.

In a small mixing bowl, combine the almond flour, sesame seeds, and parmesan cheese. Dip each chicken tender into this mixture and place on a prepared baking sheet.

Bake for 10 minutes on each side. In the meantime, in a small mixing bowl, mix the spicy mayo ingredients and set aside.

Serve chicken while still warm with spicy mayo.

Miryam's Note: These baked chicken fingers are great with the roasted vegetables on page 67.

ASIAN QUINOA SALAD

dairy-free | vegetarian | vegan | gluten-free | heart-healthy | nut-free

Yield: 4 servings

1½ cups quinoa, cooked
1 14-ounce can garbanzo beans, drained
1 cucumber, chopped
1 small onion, finely chopped
3 carrots, finely chopped
4 ounces cherry tomatoes, diced
1 ounce fresh mint, chopped

Dressing
3 tablespoons sesame oil
¼ cup rice wine vinegar
1 teaspoon matcha powder
½ teaspoon Celtic salt
¼ teaspoon crushed ground pepper

In a small bowl, add the dressing ingredients and mix thoroughly. In a large mixing bowl, add the remainder of the ingredients and combine. Add the dressing ingredients and mix thoroughly. Place salad in the refrigerator for at least 2 hours before serving.

Miryam's Note: You may add more sesame oil and rice wine vinegar depending on salad dressing preferences.

CAULIFLOWER SALAD

dairy-free | vegetarian | vegan | gluten-free | heart-healthy | nut-free

Yield: 4 servings

1 head of cauliflower, cooked and cut into florets
1 14-ounce can garbanzo beans, drained
¼ cup sunflower seeds

Dressing
3 tablespoons extra-virgin olive oil
¼ cup rice wine vinegar
1 teaspoon matcha powder
¼ teaspoon Celtic salt

In a small mixing bowl, add the dressing ingredients and mix with a fork or a wire whisk. Set aside.

In a large bowl, add the cauliflower florets, garbanzo beans, and sunflower seeds. Add the dressing and combine.

Serve immediately.

MAC AND CHEESE

nut-free | vegetarian

Yield: 6 servings

15 ounces whole wheat elbow macaroni
1 head cauliflower, chopped
2–3 tablespoons olive oil
4–6 garlic cloves, chopped
1 cup low-fat Greek plain yogurt
¼ cup organic milk

½ cup half-and-half
16 ounces mozzarella cheese, grated
½ cup parmesan cheese
1 teaspoon matcha powder
1 teaspoon Celtic salt
fresh thyme springs

Heat oven to 400 degrees Fahrenheit.

In a large pot, cook the pasta according to package instructions. When the pasta has about 5 minutes left to cook, add the cauliflower. Drain pasta and cauliflower and set aside.

In a large nonstick skillet, add the oil and garlic and cook until soft for about 30–60 seconds.

In a 9 x 13-inch baking dish, mix in the yogurt, garlic, milk, half-and-half, mozzarella and parmesan cheese, matcha powder, salt, and thyme. Incorporate the pasta with the cauliflower into this mixture and combine. Sprinkle some extra mozzarella cheese over the pasta, if desired.

Cover the baking pan with foil and bake in the preheated oven for about 20–25 minutes. To brown the top, place the baking pan under the broiler for 3–5 minutes.

Serve with some extra thyme springs.

Miryam's Note: You can choose any other combination of cheeses. Provolone cheese and gruyere work really well.

SPINACH MUSHROOM PASTA

vegetarian | nut-free

Yield: 4 servings

16 ounces spinach linguine
2 tablespoons olive oil
20 ounces fresh Portobello mushrooms, sliced
5 garlic cloves, chopped
1 cup vegetable stock
½ cup parmesan cheese

½ teaspoon matcha powder
½ teaspoon ground black pepper
½ teaspoon Celtic salt
2 tablespoons butter
fresh rosemary

Bring a large pot with water to a boil. Add the pasta and cook, stirring occasionally for 6–8 minutes. Don't cook the pasta until completely tender—it will cook further when transferring pasta into the pan.

In a large skillet over medium to high heat, add the olive oil followed by the mushrooms. Cook for 3–5 minutes until the mushrooms are tender. Add the garlic and cook for one minute until fragrant. Add the vegetable stock, parmesan cheese, matcha powder, salt, and black pepper and combine.

Add the pasta and let it cook for 2–3 minutes so the pasta will absorb some of the juice. Add the butter and sprinkle some fresh rosemary over the pasta.

Serve immediately with some extra parmesan cheese, if desired.

Miryam's Note: You can use any other pasta of your choice. Even a gluten-free version will work with this recipe.

ROASTED VEGETABLES

vegetarian | gluten-free | heart-healthy | nut-free

Yield: 6 servings

3 large red onions
4 beets
3 large parsnips
6 large potatoes
1 teaspoon paprika
1 teaspoon Celtic salt

1 teaspoon chili powder
½ teaspoon matcha powder
3 tablespoons olive oil
6 ounces goat cheese
fresh rosemary

Preheat oven to 375 degrees Fahrenheit.

Quarter the onion and beets and set aside. Cut the parsnips and potatoes into large chunks and mix with the onions and beets.

In a large roasting pan, add the vegetables, spices, and olive oil. Mix well until the spices and oil are all rubbed in into the vegetables.

Bake on the preheated oven for 35–40 minutes or until all the vegetables are tender.

Sprinkle the goat cheese and fresh rosemary leaves over the veggies and serve immediately while still warm.

Miryam's Note: You can use any other type of hearty vegetables that are in season. Roasting vegetables is very easy–pretty much any vegetable can be roasted.

OVEN-ROASTED CHICKEN FAJITAS

nut-free

Yield: 4 servings

2 pounds organic chicken
1 large red pepper
1 large green pepper
1 large onion
1 teaspoon cumin
1 teaspoon paprika

½ teaspoon thyme powder
½ teaspoon oregano powder
½ teaspoon matcha powder
½ teaspoon Celtic salt
2 tablespoons olive oil

Preheat oven to 400 degrees Fahrenheit.

Cut chicken breast into strips. Place chicken strips in a rectangular baking sheet.

Slice peppers and onion and place in a baking sheet. Add the spices and olive oil and mix well. Bake in the preheated oven for 30–35 minutes.

Serve as desired.

CREAMY KALE TOMATO PASTA

nut-free | vegetarian

Yield: 6 servings

1 pound whole wheat penne pasta
1 teaspoon arrowroot powder
½ cup almond milk
2 tablespoons olive oil
4–5 garlic cloves
1 cup heavy cream
8 ounces cherry tomatoes, sliced

10 ounces fresh kale
3 ounces goat cheese
½ teaspoon matcha powder
1 tablespoon paprika
½ teaspoon Celtic salt
¼ cup parmesan cheese

Bring a large pot of water to a boil. Add the pasta and cook, stirring occasionally until tender, 8–10 minutes.

In a small bowl, mix the arrowroot powder and milk and set aside. In a large skillet, add the olive oil and garlic and cook until fragrant, about 1 minute. Add the heavy cream, goat cheese, matcha powder, paprika, and salt to the pan and cook until the spices are well incorporated. Add the arrowroot powder mixture with sliced tomatoes and cook until the sauce is warm and thickens a bit. To the skillet, add the fresh kale and parmesan cheese followed by the cooked pasta.

Combine and serve with some extra parmesan cheese and red pepper flakes, if desired.

Miryam's Note: You can make this recipe gluten-free by using gluten-free pasta. You can also use any milk of your choice, although soy is not recommended. While I normally use almond milk, you can use regular cow's milk, as well.

CAULIFLOWER AND THYME SOUP

gluten-free | vegetarian | nut-free | heart-healthy | dairy-free | vegan

Yield: 6 servings

3 cups vegetable stock
2 teaspoons thyme powder
½ teaspoon matcha powder
1 head cauliflower

1 tablespoon olive oil
5 garlic cloves, chopped
1 teaspoon Celtic salt
1 teaspoon black ground pepper

Over medium to high heat, add the vegetable stock, thyme, and matcha powder to a large pot and bring to a boil. Add the cauliflower broken into florets and cook until the cauliflower is tender about 4–6 minutes.

In the meantime, in a small sauce pan, add the olive oil and garlic and cook until fragrant, about 1 minute.

When the cauliflower is almost tender, add the garlic, salt, and pepper and cook further for 1–2 minutes. Turn off the flame and, with an emersion blender, blend the soup until smooth.

Serve immediately.

MUSHROOM KALE CHICKEN PASTA

nut-free

Yield: 6 servings

1 pound whole wheat spaghetti
2 cups vegetable stock
½ teaspoon matcha powder
3 teaspoons arrowroot powder
2 tablespoon olive oil
2 pounds organic chicken breast, cubed

20 ounces mushrooms, sliced
6 garlic cloves, chopped
½ cup dry white wine
10 ounces fresh kale
2 tablespoons butter

Bring a large pot with water to a boil. Add the pasta and cook, stirring occasionally until tender, 8–10 minutes.

In a small bowl, mix the vegetable stock, matcha, and arrowroot powder and set aside.

In a large skillet, over medium to high heat, add the oil to the pan followed by the cubed chicken. Cook for 5 minutes until the chicken is half cooked. Add mushrooms and garlic to the pan and cook for 2–3 minutes or until the mushrooms are soft. Add wine and cook until it is reduced by half. Add the kale and stock mixture and combine for 1 minute. Turn heat off and add the cooked pasta and butter.

Combine and serve while still warm.

Miryam's Note: You can make this recipe gluten-free by using gluten-free pasta or vegetarian by omitting the chicken.

MAHI MAHI IN TOMATO SAUCE

gluten-free | nut-free | heart-healthy | dairy-free

Yield: 4 servings

3 tablespoon olive oil
1 yellow pepper, chopped
1 green pepper, chopped
1 red onion, chopped
1 pound (16 ounces) canned
   marinara sauce

1 green hot pepper, sliced
½ teaspoon Celtic salt
½ teaspoon matcha powder
1 teaspoon garlic powder
2 pounds Mahi Mahi, cut into chucks
1 cup fresh parsley

Over medium to high heat, add the olive oil to a large skillet. Add the yellow and green peppers and onion and cook for 3–5 minutes. Add the marinara sauce, hot pepper, salt, matcha powder, and garlic powder, and combine. Lower the heat to medium low and add the Mahi Mahi. Cook, stirring occasionally, for 5 minutes or until the fish is cooked.

Turn heat off and add parsley. Serve while still warm.

Miryam's Note: You can use any other firm fish of your choice; salmon works well with this recipe. You can also serve this dish over pasta, brown rice, or quinoa.

TOFU STIR-FRY

gluten-free | nut-free | heart-healthy | dairy-free |
vegan | vegetarian

Yield: 4 servings

16 ounces extra firm tofu, cubed
2 tablespoons arrowroot powder
¼ cup soy sauce
½ cup water
½ teaspoon matcha powder
1 tablespoons unrefined sugar
3 tablespoon olive oil

2 tablespoons sesame oil
2 red peppers, chopped
2 tablespoons fresh ginger, chopped
10 green onions
1 tablespoon sesame seeds
red pepper flakes, optional

In a medium bowl, mix the tofu and arrowroot powder. In a small bowl, mix the soy sauce, water, matcha powder, and sugar and set aside.

Heat a large skillet over medium to high heat. Add the olive oil and sesame oil followed by the tofu. Cook, stirring occasionally, until the tofu begins to brown around the edges, 3–4 minutes.

Add the chopped red peppers and ginger and cook further for 3–5 minutes or until the peppers are cooked. Add the soy sauce mixture and cook until thick for an extra minute. Turn heat off and add the green onions, sesame seeds, and pepper flakes if using.

Serve while still warm over brown rice, quinoa, or noodles of choice.

Miryam's Note: Make sure the soy sauce is gluten-free for a gluten-free version. You can also use cubed chicken instead of tofu.

ASPARAGUS AND TOMATO QUINOA SALAD

**gluten-free | nut-free | heart-healthy | dairy-free |
vegan | vegetarian**

Yield: 4 servings

2 tablespoons extra-virgin olive oil

12 ounces fresh asparagus

8 ounces cherry tomatoes

4 tablespoon balsamic vinegar

1½ cups quinoa, cooked

1 14-ounce can garbanzo beans, drained

½ teaspoon Celtic salt

1 teaspoon matcha powder

In a large skillet over medium to high heat, add the oil and fresh asparagus and cook for 3–5 minutes. Add the cherry tomatoes followed by the balsamic vinegar and cook for an additional 2–3 minutes or until the tomatoes begin to brown. Turn the heat off.

Add the quinoa, garbanzo beans, salt, and matcha powder and combine. Serve salad while still warm.

LENTIL AND ARUGULA SALAD

gluten-free | vegetarian | heart-healthy | nut-free

Yield: 4 servings

2 small cucumbers
4 medium radishes
7 ounces fresh arugula
¼ cup sunflower seeds
4 ounces goat cheese

Dressing
3 tablespoons Dijon mustard
3 tablespoons rice wine vinegar
3 tablespoons extra-virgin olive oil
1 tablespoon honey
½ teaspoon matcha powder

In a small mixing bowl with a wire whisk, mix the dressing ingredients and set aside.

With a grater, thinly slice the cucumbers and radishes. In a large mixing bowl, add the arugula, sunflower seeds, and crumbled goat cheese followed by the cucumbers and radishes. Add the salad dressing and mix well.

Serve immediately.

Miryam's Note: You can use any other greens of your choice. Fresh organic spinach and baby kale works rather well. To make the salad vegan, omit the goat cheese and replace the honey with maple syrup.

ASIAN CABBAGE SALAD

gluten-free | vegetarian | heart-healthy | dairy-free | vegan

Yield: 4 servings

1 small head of red cabbage
1 small head of green cabbage
5 green onions
1 red hot pepper
2 tablespoons sesame seeds

Dressing
1–2 tablespoons ginger
½ cup organic peanut butter
1 tablespoon soy sauce
2 tablespoons rice wine vinegar
2 tablespoons honey
2 tablespoons sesame oil
½ cup water
1 teaspoon matcha powder

Finely grate the red and green cabbage and add it to a large salad bowl. Chop the green onion and hot red pepper and add it to the bowl. Set aside.

Grate the ginger and add it to a medium bowl. Add the remainder of the dressing ingredients and whisk until combined.

Add the dressing to the cabbage mixture and mix thoroughly. Let the salad chill in the refrigerator for 1–2 hours before serving.

Miryam's Note: Make sure the soy sauce is gluten-free for a gluten-free version. For a vegan version, use maple syrup instead of honey.

KALE MUSHROOM FLATBREAD PIZZA

vegetarian | heart-healthy

Yield: 6 pizzas

2 tablespoons olive oil
10 ounces mushrooms, sliced
12 ounces fresh kale
16 ounces ricotta cheese

1 teaspoon matcha powder
6 whole wheat flatbreads
2 ounces goat cheese
2 red hot peppers, chopped

In a large skillet over medium to high heat, add the olive oil and mushroom and cook for 3–4 minutes or until they shrink. Add the fresh kale and toss with the mushrooms. Cook this mixture for an additional 2–3 minutes. Turn the heat off and set aside.

Place the ricotta cheese and matcha powder in a bowl and mix thoroughly. Spread the ricotta cheese over one side of each flatbread. Arrange the kale mushroom mixture over each piece of bread and sprinkle with crumbled goat cheese and chopped hot peppers.

Serve immediately.

EGG NOODLES WITH TOFU

vegetarian | heart-healthy

Yield: 4–6 servings

16 ounces egg noodles
⅓ cup reduced sodium soy sauce
1 tablespoon chile paste
½ teaspoon matcha powder
3 tablespoons sesame oil
16 extra firm tofu, cut into strips
6 ounces fresh green beans, halved

1 tablespoon ginger
4 ounces fresh bean sprouts
1 red onion, sliced
1 tablespoon sesame seeds
1 small, hot red pepper, sliced
red pepper flakes, optional

Cook egg noodles according to package instructions.

In a medium bowl with a fork or a whisk, mix the soy sauce, chile paste, and matcha powder and set aside.

Heat a large skillet over medium to high heat, add the sesame oil followed by the tofu. Cook, stirring occasionally until the tofu begins to brown around the edges, 2–3 minutes.

Add the green beans and ginger and cook for 3–5 minutes or until the green beans soften. Add the bean sprouts and cook further for 1 minute. Add the cooked noodles and soy sauce mixture and combine until the noodles are coated. Turn the heat off and sprinkle sesame seeds, sliced hot red pepper, and red pepper flakes if using.

Serve immediately.

Miryam's Note: For a vegan version, use egg-free noodles. You can also use any other vegetables of your choice, as this dish is a very versatile. You can even use chicken in place of tofu if you like.

DECADENT DESSERTS

FUDGE

gluten-free | vegetarian | heart-healthy | dairy-free | vegan

Yield: 20-24 pieces

1½ cup cashews
1 cup cocoa butter, melted
½ teaspoon Celtic salt
½ cup coconut oil, melted
2 teaspoons vanilla extract
3 teaspoons matcha powder

Soak 1 cup of cashews for 4–5 hours. Discard water.

Line a 9 x 5-inch loaf pan with foil and set aside.

Place soaked cashews in a food processor and pulse until smooth. About 3–5 minutes. Add the rest of the ingredients and mix thoroughly until well combined.

Transfer mixture to a medium mixing bowl and add the extra ½ cup cashew nuts. Combine with a spatula. Transfer the mixture to the prepared baking dish and spread evenly. Place the mixture in the freezer for 2–3 hours until it solidifies. Cut fudge into small squares and serve.

Store fudge covered in a airtight glass container in the fridge.

COCONUT ICE CREAM

gluten-free | vegetarian | dairy-free | vegan | nut-free

Yield: 4 servings

1 14-ounce can coconut cream
¼ cup maple syrup
1 tablespoon matcha powder
1 tablespoon cacao nibs, optional

Place ingredients, except cacao nibs, in a medium mixing bowl and whisk until combined. Place mixture in a freezer-safe container and freeze for at least 2 hours.

Serve with cacao nib sprinkles or as desired.

CHOCOLATE CHUNK COOKIES

gluten-free

Yield: 16 cookies

½ cup coconut oil melted
1 organic egg
½ cup unrefined sugar
2 tablespoons cocoa powder
1¼ cup brown rice flour

1 teaspoon vanilla extract
½ teaspoon matcha powder
½ teaspoon baking soda
½ cup dark chocolate chunks

Preheat oven to 350 degrees Fahrenheit. Line two baking sheets with unbleached parchment paper and set aside.

In a medium mixing bowl, add the coconut oil, egg, and sugar and whisk thoroughly until ingredients are incorporated. Alternatively you can use a stand mixer. Add the brown rice flour, cocoa powder, vanilla extract, matcha powder, baking soda, and combine.

Fold in the chocolate chunks. With a medium cookie scoop, place cookie batter onto each baking sheet about 2 inches apart. Bake for 8–10 minutes. Cool cookies on a wire rack and store in an airtight container.

BLUEBERRY CRISP

gluten-free | vegan | dairy-free | heart-healthy

Yield: 8 servings

10 ounces fresh organic blueberries
2 teaspoons arrowroot powder
1 cup gluten-free rolled oats
½ cup pecan halves
½ cup almond meal
⅓ cup unsweetened shredded coconut

¼ teaspoon cinnamon
1 teaspoon vanilla extract
⅓ coconut oil, melted
⅓ cup maple syrup
1 teaspoon matcha powder

Preheat your oven to 350 degrees Fahrenheit. In a round 9-inch pie dish, add the blueberries and arrowroot powder and mix thoroughly. Set aside.

In a large mixing bowl, mix the rest of the ingredients until you obtain a cohesive mixture. Spread this mixture evenly over the blueberries.

Bake for 25–30 minutes or until the top starts to brown. Turn the oven off and let the crisp cool in the oven for 30 minutes.

Serve warm or as desired.

Miryam's Note: You can also use frozen organic blueberries previously thawed out as well as any other fresh fruit of your choice.

FLOURLESS BROWNIES

gluten-free | dairy-free

Yield: 12 pieces

3 organic eggs
½ cup sugar
2 teaspoons vanilla extract
½ cup coconut oil, melted
6 ounces dark chocolate

¾ cup cocoa powder
¼ teaspoon Celtic salt
½ teaspoon baking powder
1 teaspoon matcha powder
⅓ cup walnuts, chopped

Preheat oven to 350 degrees Fahrenheit. Line an 8 x 8-inch square baking dish with unbleached parchment paper and set aside.

In a mixing bowl add eggs, sugar, vanilla, and coconut oil, and with a wire whisk beat until ingredients are combined. Alternatively, you can use a stand mixer.

Place the dark chocolate in a microwave-safe dish and microwave at 30-second intervals, stirring in between until the chocolate is melted.

Add the melted chocolate to the previous egg mixture and combine. Add the cocoa powder, salt and baking powder to the bowl. With a spatula, fold until all is incorporated. The mixture will be thick. Place batter in the prepared pan and sprinkle the batter with the chopped walnuts.

Bake for 25–30 minutes or until a tester inserted in the center comes out clean. Let the brownies cool on a wire rack for at least 30 minutes and cut into squares.

BAKED DONUTS

Yield: 10 donuts

2 organic eggs
⅓ cup plain Greek yogurt
½ cup unrefined sugar
½ cup almond milk
2 tablespoons olive oil
1¾ cups whole wheat pastry flour
1 teaspoon baking powder
½ teaspoon baking soda
1 tablespoon matcha powder

Glaze
1 teaspoon coconut oil
½ cup dark chocolate chips
cacao nibs, optional
pistachios, crushed, optional

Preheat oven to 325 degrees Fahrenheit. Generously grease two medium donut pans and set aside.

In a bowl, whisk eggs, yogurt, sugar, milk, and oil. Add flour, baking powder, baking soda, and matcha powder. Whisk until combined. Fill each donut hole two-thirds full.

Bake for 18–22 minutes or until a tester comes out clean. Cool donuts in the pan for about 15–20 minutes and move them to a wire rack to cool completely.

While the donuts are cooling, using a microwave-safe dish, melt the coconut oil with the dark chocolate chips in 30-second intervals, stirring often until the chocolate is melted. Dip each donut in the melted chocolate and sprinkle some chopped pistachios and cacao nibs, if desired. Store donuts on a cake stand for up to two days.

Miryam's Note: Make sure you grease the donut pans generously otherwise they will be hard to remove from the baking pan and may break in the process. I also use a butter knife to help me remove the donuts from the pan.

BROWNIE MUG CAKE

gluten-free | dairy-free

Yield: 2 mug cakes

3 tablespoons egg whites
3 tablespoons maple syrup
½ cup almond milk
¼ cup dark chocolate chips
2 tablespoons coconut oil

3 tablespoons coconut flour
¼ teaspoon baking powder
½ teaspoon matcha powder
¼ teaspoon instant coffee powder
pinch of Celtic salt

Place egg whites, maple syrup, and almond milk in a mixing bowl and with a wire whisk mix until combined. Melt the chocolate and coconut oil in a microwave safe bowl at 30-second intervals, stirring in between until the chocolate is melted.

Add the melted chocolate and coconut oil to the batter with a spatula and fold in. Add the coconut flour, baking powder, matcha powder, instant coffee, and salt and fold with the spatula.

Divide batter among 2–3 mugs, depending on how big they are, and microwave on high for 4–5 minutes. Serve immediately with some heavy cream or ice cream.

Miryam's Note: Depending on microwave power, you may need more or less time for the brownie mug to cook. The strength of my microwave was 800 watts and it took about 4½ minutes.

FROZEN POPSICLES

gluten-free | dairy-free | vegan

Yield: 12 popsicles

1 14-ounce can coconut cream
½ cup almond milk
¼ cup maple syrup
¼ cup unsweetened shredded coconut
2 teaspoons matcha powder

Toppings
6 ounces dark chocolate chips
¼ cup raw pistachios, chopped
¼ cup goji berries
1 tablespoon unsweetened shredded coconut

Place all the ingredients in a blender and pulse until you obtain a homogenous mixture. Divide the mixture into your preferred popsicle molds and freeze for at least 3–4 hours.

Melt the chocolate in a microwave-safe bowl in 30-second intervals until completely melted. Before serving, dip each popsicle in the melted chocolate and sprinkle with raw pistachios, berries, and shredded coconut.

Miryam's Note: You can use any other toppings of your choice or leave the popsicles topping-free.

NO-BAKE CASHEW BANANA PIE

gluten-free | dairy-free | vegan

Yield: 8 slices

Crust
¾ cup dates, pitted
½ cup rolled oats
½ cup cashews
1 tablespoon cocoa powder
2 tablespoons coconut oil, melted

Filling
16 ounces cashew butter
3 large ripe bananas
2 teaspoons real vanilla paste or extract
2 tablespoons maple syrup
2 tablespoons coconut oil
1 teaspoon matcha powder

Topping
⅓ cup cashews, chopped
⅓ cup dark chocolate chips
2 tablespoons coconut oil

Line a 9-inch round cake pan with unbleached parchment paper and set aside.

Add the crust ingredients to your food processor and process until smooth. Add this mixture to the prepared lined baking pan and press until with a spatula even on all sides.

Place the filling ingredients in the food processor and pulse until you obtain a homogenous mixture. Add the filling on top of the crust and freeze pie until solid for at least 4–6 hours.

When ready to eat, sprinkle the cashews over the pie. Place the chocolate chips and coconut oil in a microwave-safe dish and microwave at 30-second intervals, stirring in between, until the chocolate has melted. Drizzle the chocolate over the cashews and serve.

You may have to let the pie sit at room temperature for 10–15 minutes to be able to slice. Store leftover pie in the freezer and thaw for 10–15 minutes before eating.

Miryam's Note: To make the pie gluten-free, use gluten-free rolled oats, and to make it vegan, use vegan chocolate chips.

WHITE CHOCOLATE MOUSSE

Yield: 4 servings

4 ounces white chocolate
2 tablespoons maple syrup
2 cups heavy cream
½ cup Greek yogurt
2 teaspoons matcha powder
2 tablespoons pistachios, chopped

In a microwavable-safe dish melt the chocolate in 30- to 45-second intervals, stirring in between until melted. Set aside.

Place maple syrup and heavy cream in a medium mixing bowl and, with a handheld mixer, beat the heavy cream until it resembles soft peaks. Alternatively, you can use a stand mixer. Carefully fold in the Greek yogurt followed by the melted chocolate and matcha powder until the chocolate and yogurt are incorporated.

Divide mixture between four individual glasses. Place mousse glasses in the refrigerator for at least 2–3 hours to set. Garnish with chopped pistachios before serving.

NO-BAKE COCONUT MACAROONS

gluten-free | dairy-free | vegan | nut-free | vegetarian

Yield: 20–25 coconut macaroons

1 cup dark chocolate
1 cup unsweetened shredded coconut
1 teaspoon matcha powder
2–3 tablespoons coconut oil, melted

Place chocolate in a microwavable dish and melt in 20- to 30-second intervals, stirring in between.

Place shredded coconut, matcha powder, and melted coconut oil in a small mixing bowl and combine. Place 1 tablespoon of melted chocolate into a silicone square baking mold followed by 1–2 teaspoons of the coconut mixture. Press with your fingers and let it sit until the chocolate has hardened. Repeat this step until you don't have any chocolate left.

Let the coconut macaroons set. For a speedy setting time, place the silicone mold in the refrigerator for 30 minutes. Remove coconut macaroons from mold and serve.

Miryam's Note: For a vegan version, use dairy-free chocolate.

WHOLE WHEAT STICKY BUNS

Yield: 6 large buns

Dough

2½–3 cups whole wheat pastry flour

⅓ cup unrefined sugar

2½ teaspoons instant rapid yeast (1 package)

¼ teaspoon Celtic salt

¾ cup water

3 tablespoons coconut oil, melted

1 organic egg

Filling

⅓ cup sugar

1 teaspoon matcha powder

3 teaspoons cinnamon

1 egg white

Topping

¼ cup maple syrup

1 tablespoon pumpkin seeds

1 tablespoon goji berries

Line an 8-inch round baking pan with unbleached parchment paper and set aside.

Combine the 2½ cups flour, sugar, dry yeast, and salt in a large mixing bowl and stir until combined. Place water and coconut oil in a microwave-safe bowl and microwave in 15-second increments until warm but not hot to the touch. Add to the flour mixture in the bowl, followed by the whole egg.

Beat 2 minutes at medium speed with a hand or stand mixer. If you find the dough still too sticky, add a small amount of flour at a time until the dough is no longer sticky to the touch.

Knead dough on a lightly floured surface until smooth and elastic and until dough springs back when lightly pressed with 2 fingers, about 4–6 minutes. Place the dough in a medium

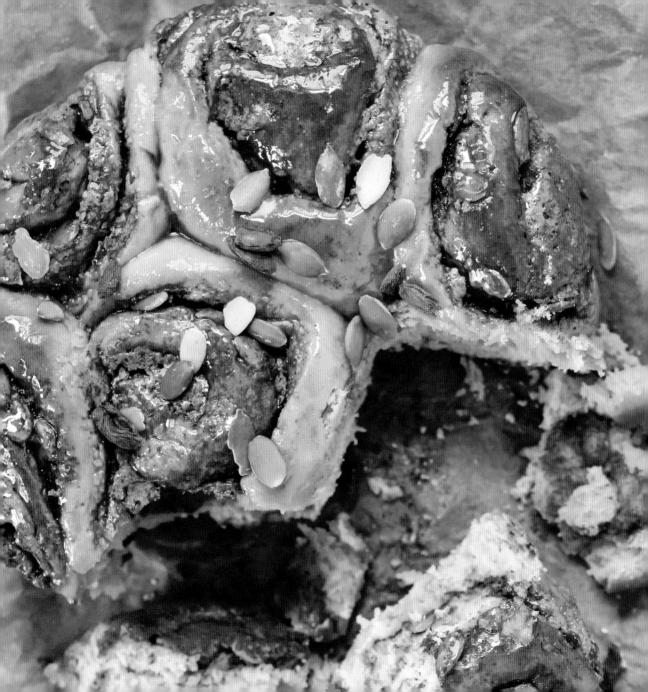

bowl previously greased with some coconut oil and cover with a tea towel. Let it rest for 10 minutes.

For the filling, combine sugar, matcha powder, cinnamon, and egg white in a small bowl. Set aside.

Roll dough into a 15 x 10-inch rectangle using a rolling pin. Spread the filling mixture over dough, stopping a half inch from the edges. Roll up the dough and pinch seams to seal. Cut dough into 6 equal pieces and place on the prepared baking pan. Place buns cut-side down. Cover with a tea towel and let it rise in a warm place until doubled in size, about 1 hour.

Preheat oven to 350 degrees Fahrenheit. Bake for 25–30 minutes or until rolls are golden brown. Cool on wire rack for 10–15 minutes. Pour maple syrup over the buns and sprinkle the pumpkin seeds and goji berries. Serve while they are still warm.

Miryam's Note: You can use any other nuts of your choice. I have used walnut and pecan before and they're great!

CHOCOLATE CAKE WITH HEAVY CREAM FROSTING

gluten-free | vegetarian

Yield: 6 servings

3 organic eggs
½ cup almond milk
½ cup coconut oil
2 teaspoons vanilla extract
½ cup unrefined sugar
2 cups almond flour
⅓ cup coconut flour
2 tablespoons cocoa powder
½ teaspoon matcha powder
½ teaspoon aluminum free baking soda
1 teaspoon baking powder

Frosting
1 cup heavy cream
3 tablespoons maple syrup
½ tablespoon matcha powder

Preheat your oven to 350 degrees Fahrenheit. Line the bottom of an 8-inch round cake pan with unbleached parchment paper. Grease the sides with coconut oil and set aside.

In a medium mixing bowl, add the eggs, milk, coconut oil, vanilla extract, and sugar and whisk until combined. Add the flours, cocoa powder, matcha powder, baking soda, and baking powder and mix thoroughly.

Pour batter over the prepared pan and bake for 35–40 minutes or until a cake tester comes out clean. Let the cake cool in the pan for 20–30 minutes. Remove cake from the pan and cool completely on a wire rack.

When the cake is cool, in a mixing bowl mix the heavy cream, matcha powder, and maple syrup until the heavy cream forms soft peaks. Top the cake with the heavy cream mixture and serve.

Store cake in the fridge for up to 2 days.

Miryam's Note: For a dairy-free option, you can use coconut cream in place of heavy cream.

CREAM BARS

gluten-free | dairy-free | vegan | vegetarian | heart-healthy

Yield: 16 bars

Crust
2 cups raw cashews
1½ cup dates
2 tablespoons water
1 teaspoon matcha powder

Filling
1 14-ounce can coconut
   cream
1 teaspoon matcha powder
1 teaspoon vanilla extract
¼ cup maple syrup

Topping
⅓ cup coconut oil
⅓ cup cocoa powder
⅓ tablespoon maple syrup

Line an 8 x 8-inch square baking pan with unbleached parchment paper. Set aside.

Place the crust ingredients in your food processor and pulse until combined or until the mixture comes together. If the crust doesn't come together, don't be afraid of adding more water. With a spatula, press evenly into the prepared baking pan.

Blend the filling ingredients in the food processor until smooth and spread evenly over the crust. Freeze the bars for at least 2 hours before pouring the chocolate topping over them.

For the topping, place the ingredients in a small bowl and microwave 30 seconds to 1 minutes or until the coconut oil is melted. With a fork, mix the topping ingredients and pour over the middle layer making sure to spread it evenly.

Freeze bars until firm. To serve, let the bars thaw at room temperature for 10–15 minutes and cut as desired.

Miryam's Note: You can use any other nuts of your choice for the crust. Almonds also work very well.

NO-BAKE PISTACHIO AND PUMPKIN COOKIES

gluten-free | dairy-free | vegan | vegetarian | heart-healthy

Yield: 12 cookies

Cookies
1 cup pistachios
1 cup pumpkin seeds
1 cup unsweetened shredded coconut
¼ cup maple syrup
1 teaspoon matcha powder
2 tablespoons water
1 teaspoon vanilla extract

Filling
1 cup unsweetened shredded coconut
¼ cup almond flour
2 tablespoons maple syrup
1 teaspoon vanilla extract
2 tablespoons coconut oil

Place the cookie ingredients in your food processor and pulse until combined or until the mixture comes together. Place mixture between plastic wrap and, with a rolling pin, roll the cookie dough flat—about ½-inch thick. With a round cookie cutter, cut cookies until you have no more dough. Place the cookies in the freezer for 5–10 minutes to harden.

In a microwave-safe bowl, melt the coconut oil and set aside. Place the shredded coconut in your food processor and pulse until you have a powder consistency. Place the coconut powder in a medium mixing bowl and add the rest of the filling ingredients. With a spoon, mix together until you obtain a paste.

Take the cookies out of the freezer and, with a small spatula, place about 1–2 tablespoons of the filling over one cookie. Place another cookie on top of the filling, creating a sandwich effect, and press. Repeat this method until you have no more cookies.

Store cookies in the refrigerator.

Miryam's Note: You can dip them in chocolate if you like.

APPLE WALNUT BUNDT CAKE

Yield: 12-16 slices

2 organic eggs
1 cup unrefined sugar
¾ cup coconut oil, melted
2 teaspoons vanilla extract
1 cup almond milk
2 cups whole wheat pastry flour
2 teaspoons baking powder

1 teaspoon matcha powder
2 teaspoons cinnamon powder
½ teaspoon baking soda
3 organic apples, cubed
⅓ cup golden raisins
1 cup walnuts, chopped

Preheat your oven to 350 degrees Fahrenheit. Grease and flour a bundt cake generously. Set aside.

In a large mixing bowl, add the eggs, sugar, coconut oil, vanilla, and milk. Whisk or use a stand mixer if you have one. Add the flour, baking soda, matcha powder, cinnamon, and baking powder and combine. With a spatula, fold in the chopped apples, golden raisins, and chopped walnuts.

Pour the mixture in the prepared bundt cake and bake for 50–60 minutes or until a tester comes out clean.

Cool cake in the pan for at least 15–20 minutes before unmolding. Transfer the cake to a wire rack to cool completely.

Miryam's Note: You can drizzle some caramel sauce, chocolate sauce, or serve the apple walnut bundt cake as is. I like it with maple syrup.

DARK CHOCOLATE TRUFFLES

gluten-free | vegetarian

Yield: 20–25 truffles

12 ounces dark chocolate
1 teaspoon vanilla extract
¾ cup heavy cream

½ teaspoon matcha powder
matcha to coat
raw chopped pistachios to coat, optional

Place the chocolate in a medium mixing bowl and add the vanilla extract. Set aside.

Over medium to low flame, in a sauce pan, add the heavy cream until it starts to bubble around the rim of the pan, but make sure it does not boil. Add the hot heavy cream to the chocolate and whisk until the chocolate melts. This will take 2–3 minutes.

Cover the mixture and place it in the fridge until set, at least 4 hours. After the chocolate has set and hardened, use a small cookie scoop or tablespoon to scoop out little pieces of the chocolate mixture and form balls between the palms of your hands.

Place matcha powder in one plate and chopped pistachios (if using) on another. Roll the chocolate balls in the matcha powder or pistachios.

Keep truffles refrigerated until it is time to serve.

Miryam's Note: For a vegan version, use coconut milk in place of heavy cream and choose a vegan chocolate instead of dark chocolate. You can also add any other flavor of choice such as lemon or orange extract.

MEAL PLANS

With the recipes provided in this cookbook, you can plan your menu for up to four weeks. Here are two weeks of samples. Feel free to adapt them to fit your taste, preferences, and lifestyle. I included a mid-morning snack, which you can place between lunch and dinner or ignore completely if you like. Because I don't count calories (except for illness purposes and special diets like for diabetics), these weekly menu plans are not designed for you to lose weight but do promote healthy eating. As for portion sizes, each recipe was provided with the yields. Stick to one serving unless noted or if you have a very active lifestyle. Use common sense here!

Week One

DAY	Breakfast	Snack	Lunch	Dinner
Monday	Granola with plain Greek yogurt (pg 3)	1 Energy Bar (pg 27)	Cauliflower Salad (pg 60)	Spinach Mushroom Pasta (pg 64) and 2 Chocolate Chunk Cookies (pg 95)
Tuesday	Overnight Oats (pg 7)	2–3 Energy Truffles (pg 23)	Roasted Veggies (pg 67) with Cauliflower Thyme Soup (pg 72)	Oven-Roasted Chicken Fajitas (pg 68) and 1 Pistachio and Pumpkin Cookie (pg 121)
Thursday	Mango Protein Smoothie (pg 4)	2–3 Lemon Coconut Bites (pg 35)	Curried Coconut Broccoli Soup (pg 52) with 1 Kale Mushroom Flatbread Pizza (pg 87)	Asian Quinoa Salad (pg 59) and 1 serving 'Nana Ice Cream (pg 24)
Friday	Energizing Smoothie (pg 31)	2–3 Energy Truffles (pg 23)	Asian Cabbage Salad (pg 84) with 1 Kale Mushroom Flatbread Pizza (pg 87)	Tofu Stir-Fry (pg 79) and 1 Frozen Popsicle (pg 104)
Saturday	Breakfast Parfait (pg 20)	1 Energy Bar (pg 27)	Lentil and Arugula Salad (pg 83)	Mushroom Kale Chicken Pasta (pg 75)
Sunday	Breakfast Smoothie Bowl (pg 8)	2–3 Lemon Coconut Bites (pg 35)	Roasted Veggies (pg 67) with Cauliflower Thyme Soup (pg 72)	Quinoa Burger with Matcha Habanero Mayo (pg 51) and 1 piece Flourless Brownie (pg 99)

Week Two

DAY	Breakfast	Snack	Lunch	Dinner
Monday	1 Muffin (pg 19) and 1 glass of organic milk of choice	1–2 Sesame Squares (pg 39)	Noodle Salad with Asian Vinaigrette (pg 48)	Barley Risotto (pg 44) and 1 serving of Blueberry Crisp (pg 96)
Tuesday	Breakfast Frittata (pg 11)	2–3 Energy Truffles (pg 23)	Cauliflower and Thyme Soup (pg 72)	Roasted Vegetables (pg 67) with Baked Chicken Fingers (pg 56)
Thursday	1 Muffin (pg 19) and 1 glass of organic milk of choice	2–3 Energy Truffles (pg 23)	Lentil and Arugula Salad (pg 83)	Mushroom Kale Chicken Pasta (pg 75) and 1 piece of Blueberry Crisp (pg 96)
Friday	Mango Protein Smoothie (pg 4)	1–2 Sesame Squares (pg 39)	Asparagus and Tomato Quinoa Salad (pg 80)	Fish Curry (pg 47) and 1 piece of Fudge (pg 91)
Saturday	Breakfast Frittata (pg 11)	1 Energy Bar (pg 27)	Cauliflower and Thyme Soup (pg 72)	Mac and Cheese (pg 63) and 1 Frozen Popsicle (pg 104)
Sunday	Breakfast Smoothie Bowl (pg 8)	1 serving 'Nana Ice Cream (pg 24)	Lentil and Arugula Salad (pg 83)	Kale Mushroom Flatbread Pizza (pg 87)

Full disclosure: most of my equipment is purchased through Amazon.com. In this resource list, I won't give you an extensive number of equipment pieces—the bare essentials I can't personally live without. This is the equipment I use in my kitchen almost every day.

You already have your conventional pots and pans, measuring spoons and cups, and mixing bowls—staples in every kitchen, so I won't go into detail about those. What I would like to emphasize is that I never buy plastic. Even when it comes to using plastic wrap, I use beeswax-coated cloth alternatives. They're a bit more expensive but worth the investment.

I also use unbleached parchment paper when baking and lining cookie sheets and baking pans, and I also prefer recycled aluminum foil. These are readily available at most supermarkets, but if you can't get them for some reason, try an online store.

I never, ever use foam containers of any kind, as these contain dioxins that are a highly toxic compound produced as a by-product in some manufacturing processes. They are known to be carcinogenic, can cause reproductive and developmental problems, can damage the immune system, and may interfere with hormones.

Equipment

Food Processor

Seek out a good food processor. I have found certain brands to be better over others—Cuisinart as well as KitchenAid are great. A good food processor will run you at least $100, and anything below that will end up burning the motor pretty fast so don't waste your money on cheap ones. A food processor should have a minimum of a seven-cup capacity, but ideally you should own one with a capacity of nine to thirteen cups.

Blender

I use my blender almost every day. While you can buy a Blendtec or a Vitamix, these are quite expensive; however, they are worth the investment. If you can afford them, go for it. Otherwise, KitchenAid makes some great ones that are one-third of the price.

Rice Maker

Many of my readers don't think a rice maker is necessary but, with the amount of rice and quinoa my family eats, a rice maker is a godsend in my kitchen. A decent rice maker will run you about $30. It is fairly inexpensive and makes it so easy to cook these grains. For me, it's a no-brainer, but if you still would like to cook rice and quinoa the conventional way, that's totally fine.

Storage

All my storage containers are made of glass. I do not use any plastic or foam containers due to their toxic composition. I know Ikea is worldwide, and I have quite a few glass jars from them that are quite economical. I have had some luck at dollar stores, too.

Equipment Suppliers and Specialty Ingredients

Popular Sites

Amazon | www.amazon.com
Cooking.com | www.cooking.com
Williams-Sonoma | www.williams-sonoma.com
Sur La Table | www.surlatable.com
Weck Jars | www.weckjars.com
Pyrex | www.pyrex.com

Matcha

Don't purchase matcha just anywhere. Make sure it is from a reputable source. Matcha powder should be in tin containers or sealed packages, never see-through. Once you have opened the container, remember to keep it refrigerated, otherwise it will oxidize rapidly and lose its flavor and nutritional properties.

My Favorite Matcha Brands

Highest quality: DoMatcha Green Tea, Organic Matcha, 1.0-Ounce Tin *(For drinking and raw desserts)*

Premium grade: Matcha Green Tea Powder - ORGANIC - All Day Energy *(For cooking and baking)*

You can find more resources here:

Matcha and More | www.matchaandmore.com
Matcha Source | www.matchasource.com
Teavana | www.teavana.com
Aiya Matcha | www.aiyamatcha.com
Republic of Tea | www.republicoftea.com

Specialty Food (grains, flours, and superfoods)

You will find an array of different products on these sites. They not only offer grains and flours, but also dried beans and legumes and other superfoods such as chia seeds, dried fruits, nuts, seeds, and much more.

Sites

Bob's Red Mill | www.bobsredmill.com
Nuts.com | www.nuts.com
Navita Naturals | http://navitanaturals.com

National Grocery Chains

Trader Joe's
Whole Foods
Safeway
Local Harvest

CONVERSION CHARTS

Metric and Imperial Conversions

(These conversions are rounded for convenience)

Ingredient	Cups/Tablespoons/Teaspoons	Ounces	Grams/Milliliters
Butter	1 cup=16 tablespoons= 2 sticks	8 ounces	230 grams
Cream cheese	1 tablespoon	0.5 ounce	14.5 grams
Cheese, shredded	1 cup	4 ounces	110 grams
Cornstarch	1 tablespoon	0.3 ounce	8 grams
Flour, all-purpose	1 cup/1 tablespoon	4.5 ounces/0.3 ounce	125 grams/8 grams
Flour, whole wheat	1 cup	4 ounces	120 grams
Fruit, dried	1 cup	4 ounces	120 grams
Fruits or veggies, chopped	1 cup	5 to 7 ounces	145 to 200 grams
Fruits or veggies, puréed	1 cup	8.5 ounces	245 grams
Honey, maple syrup, or corn syrup	1 tablespoon	0.75 ounce	20 grams
Liquids: cream, milk, water, or juice	1 cup	8 fluid ounces	240 milliliters
Oats	1 cup	5.5 ounces	150 grams
Salt	1 teaspoon	0.2 ounces	6 grams
Spices: cinnamon, cloves, ginger, or nutmeg (ground)	1 teaspoon	0.2 ounce	5 milliliters
Sugar, brown, firmly packed	1 cup	7 ounces	200 grams
Sugar, white	1 cup/1 tablespoon	7 ounces/0.5 ounce	200 grams/12.5 grams
Vanilla extract	1 teaspoon	0.2 ounce	4 grams

oven temperatures

Fahrenheit	Celcius	Gas Mark
225°	110°	¼
250°	120°	½
275°	140°	1
300°	150°	2
325°	160°	3
350°	180°	4
375°	190°	5
400°	200°	6
425°	220°	7
450°	230°	8

ABOUT THE AUTHOR

Miryam Quinn-Doblas MS, RD, is a registered dietitian, recipe developer, photographer, and the creator of EatGood4Life.com. Her blog focuses on healthy food made from scratch, as she is passionate about the importance of optimal nutrition. Born and raised in Spain, Miryam lives in Westfield, New Jersey, where she is studying to become a physician's assistant.

Follow Miryam

www.eatgood4life.com

Facebook | https://www.facebook.com/pages/Eat-Good-4-Life/
Instagram | https://instagram.com/eatgoodforlife/
Pinterest | https://www.pinterest.com/eatgood4life/
Twitter | https://twitter.com/EatGood4Life

INDEX